KANSAS CITY ROYALS

2015 WORLD SERIES CHAMPIONS

Nicky Brillowski, Book and Cover Design

ISBN: 978-1-940056-36-4

Printed in the United States of America
KCI Sports Publishing   3340 Whiting Avenue, Suite 5   Stevens Point, WI 54481
Phone: 1-800-697-3756   Fax: 715-344-2668
www.kcisports.com

CONTENTS

Kansas City Royals catcher Drew Butera, left, and Wade Davis, right, celebrate as the rest of the team rushes out to join them. *AP Photo*

ROYALS LOOK TO BUILD OFF 2014

Kansas City Royals hitting coach Dale Sveum talks hitting with Mike Moustakas during batting practice prior to a spring training baseball game. *AP Photo*

That old, familiar baseball refrain made famous by fans of the Brooklyn Dodgers took on an entirely different meaning for the Kansas City Royals this offseason.

No longer was "Wait 'til next year!" the battle cry of a beleaguered franchise grasping at hope. The slogan had become quite literal: After snapping a 29-year playoff drought with a trip to the World Series, the Royals wanted to keep right on playing.

"We came as close as you can to winning a world championship," manager Ned Yost said, "and when you don't do it, it leaves a taste in your mouth. It's something you strive to do, and I think everyone in the locker room will tell you they want to finish this thing off."

Most of the faces will be the same as pitchers and catchers report to the Royals' spring training home in Surprise, Arizona, and position players begin to trickle in ahead of next week's first full-squad workout. But the usual business cycle of

baseball has resulted in a few notable changes, including the departure of two organizational cornerstones.

The first was James Shields. The second was Billy Butler.

Shields' arrival in a trade from Tampa Bay brought with him a winning attitude. He changed the clubhouse culture. And while the staff ace struggled in the playoffs, it's hard to argue that Kansas City would have been there without him.

The frugal Royals were not expected to make a competitive offer for him, making it a foregone conclusion that Shields would be pitching elsewhere this season. He signed a $75 million, four-year deal with San Diego.

There were higher hopes that the Royals could keep Butler, their longtime designated hitter. But after a down season, the club declined its $12.5 million option, and discussions on a new deal

fizzled. Butler signed a $30 million, three-year deal with Oakland.

The Royals hardly stashed their saved cash, though. In a sign that owner David Glass was not content with merely reaching Game 7 of the World Series last year, he gave general manager Dayton Moore the green light on a free-agent splurge.

Moore moved quickly to fill his vacant spot in the starting rotation by signing right-hander Edinson Volquez to a $20 million, two-year deal. He filled the DH spot by signing veteran Kendrys Morales to a $17 million, two-year deal. And he added a bit of power by signing outfielder Alex Rios to an $11 million contract.

Then, Moore gambled on the medical marvel of Tommy John surgery.

He resigned reliever Luke Hochevar, coming off his first elbow ligament replacement, to a $10 million, two-year deal. Then the GM signed former

Braves pitcher Kris Medlen, coming off his second such surgery, to an $8.5 million, two-year pact.

Throw in some hefty raises for All-Star closer Greg Holland and other holdovers through contract increases and salary arbitration, and Moore has pushed the Royals' payroll well over $100 million for the first time.

"We feel like we've had a strong offseason," he said. "The success of our team in 2014 is obviously due to our homegrown players, players that were on the roster prior, and they all stepped up and did a terrific job for us in September and into the postseason. So we did everything we could in the offseason to make sure our defense and pitching remained strong."

Yes, it was defense and pitching that carried Kansas City on its magical autumn run. That won't change this year, regardless of so many new faces.

Gold Glove catcher Salvador Perez is back. So are fellow Gold Glove winners Alex Gordon in left field and Eric Hosmer at first base, and defensive dynamos in Alcides Escobar at shortstop, Lorenzo Cain in center field and Omar Infante at second base.

The big question is whether the run production will be there this season.

The Royals hit the fewest homers in the majors by a wide margin last season, and it often was a chore to scratch out a single run. They are banking on the arrival of Rios and Morales along with the continued growth of their young core to help with that area.

If all goes according to their plan, the Royals believe they have enough to go one win further than last year.■

Kansas City Royals right fielder
Alex Rios hits a three-run home
run during the seventh inning.
AP Photo

APRIL 6, 2015   KAUFFMAN STADIUM   KANSAS CITY, MISSOURI
KC ROYALS 10 • CHICAGO WHITE SOX 1

ROYALS ROUT WHITE SOX 10-1 IN SEASON OPENER

Kansas City Royals starting pitcher Yordano Ventura delivers to a Chicago White Sox batter during the first inning on opening day.
AP Photo

Opening days are all about optimism and for Kansas City fans there was a lot of it floating around Kaufmann Stadium Monday afternoon.

The Royals quest for a return trip to the World Series got off on the right foot as Yordano Ventura pitched six-plus solid innings and Alex Rios had a three-run homer as Kansas City routed the Chicago White Sox 10-1.

The defending American League champions scored runs in six of the nine innings and never trailed to open the season with a victory for the first time in seven years. Jeff Samardzija took the loss for the White Sox after allowing five earned runs on six hits.

Ventura went down with a thumb cramp after throwing a strike to Adam LaRoche and was replaced by Kelvin Herrera. He will be evaluated later this week, but Royals manager Ned Yost said he does not anticipate the hard-throwing righty missing a start.

"I felt the thumb lock up on me," Ventura said, with teammate Jeremy Guthrie translating. "My first thought, it was something really bad, but I'm really happy that it's not. I'm not concerned about it at all. It's just a cramp, though, but it surprised me."

Chicago White Sox Micah Johnson (7) is tagged out by Kansas City Royals first baseman Eric Hosmer (35) during the sixth inning. *AP Photo*

Ventura just recently agreed to a $23 million, five-year contract. Ryan Madson pitched a scoreless ninth for the Royals, his first big league appearance since Sept. 28, 2011.

Salvador Perez opened the scoring in the second inning with a double to right field that made it 1-0. Lorenzo Cain made it 2-0 with an RBI hit of his own and then he scored on a wild pitch by Samardzija to up the lead to three.

Mike Moustakas made it 4-0 in the bottom of

the fifth with a solo shot but Jose Abreu countered with a seventh-inning blast for the Sox to cut the lead to three.

But the bottom dropped out for the White Sox in the seventh. Alex Gordon's two-run single pushed the lead to 6-1 before Alex Rios delivered the big blow. Rios, a former White Sox outfielder, smacked his three-run homer off Kyle Drabek to put the game out of reach. Rios finished with three hits and three RBI in his Royals debut.

"I was trying to put a good swing on the ball and when you do that good things happen," Rios said.

Eric Hosmer finished the scoring with an RBI single in the 8th off Drabek to make it 10-1 and cool some of the national pundit's preseason enthusiasm for the Sox for at least a day.

After an exhilarating postseason run last year that ended with a Game 7 loss to San Francisco in the World Series, the Royals were looking to get off to a fast start in 2015.

Alcides Escobar and Moustakas, the Royals first two hitters, went a combined 4 for 7 with two walks and scored five runs.

"The numbers don't matter," Moustakas said. "We just find a way to win and at the end of the day the numbers will be there."■

Kansas City Royals' third baseman Mike Moustakas at bat. *AP Photo*

MAY 15, 2015 · KAUFFMAN STADIUM · KANSAS CITY, MISSOURI
KC ROYALS 12 • NEW YORK YANKEES 1

ROYALS POWER PAST YANKEES

Kansas City Royals pitcher Chris Young throws during the first inning. *AP Photo*

The Royals were a couple of weeks into spring training and veteran right-hander Chris Young was still on the market when general manager Dayton Moore approached manager Ned Yost one day and asked whether they should try signing him.

Yost spent a few seconds recalling the way Young shut down the Royals last season, when he was with Seattle, and replied: "Heck yeah. Let's go get him."

Signed to provide bullpen support, Young made another strong case to have a permanent spot in the rotation Friday night. He held down the Yankees into the sixth inning, and backed by plenty of offense from Lorenzo Cain and Kendrys Morales, helped Kansas City to a 12-1 victory.

"I just tried to hold the game close and the guys came through," Young said.

Cain had a career-high five RBIs, Morales drove in three more runs and just about everyone in the

Kansas City Royals' Omar Infante (14) is safe at third base for an RBI triple during the sixth inning. *AP Photo*

Kansas City Royals' Lorenzo Cain, foreground, moves to avoid getting wet as Salvador Perez, left, douses Mike Moustakas, right.
AP Photo

Kansas City lineup took their shots against Yankees starter Michael Pineda. The result was a dominant win to open a three-game set between division leaders.

"We swung the bat well as a team tonight," Cain said. "That's all you can ask for."

Young (3-0) allowed just four hits and two walks over 5 2/3 innings in his third solid spot start. The 6-foot-10 veteran is replacing injured Jason Vargas in the rotation.

Pineda (5-1), coming off a masterful 16-strikeout performance against Baltimore, only struck out one while matching a career worst with 10 hits allowed. Pineda hung tough through the first five innings, the only damage an RBI single by Cain in the first inning and a sacrifice fly by the Royals outfielder in the fourth.

Brian McCann had a sacrifice fly for New York in the top of the fourth inning.

Everything unraveled for the AL East-leading Yankees in the fifth, though. The Royals sent 11 batters to the plate, pounded out six hits and churned through Pineda and two relievers.

Omar Infante and Paulo Orlando drove in runs to start the onslaught, and Cain added a two-run single off Justin Wilson later in the inning. By the time Morales and Alex Gordon drove in runs, Yankees manager Joe Girardi was getting fatigued walking to the mound.

Jose Ramirez, just recalled from Triple-A Scranton/Wilkes-Barre, finally got the Yankees out of the inning. But by then, the AL Central-leading Royals had pushed their lead to 8-1.

The only drama left was whether Mike Moustakas would hit for the cycle.

The Kansas City third baseman tripled, doubled and singled his first three times at bat. He grounded out in the sixth, but brought a crowd of 34,584 to its feet when he sent a fly ball down the left-field line in the seventh that bounced just a few feet from the top of the wall.

He wound up with an RBI double, giving him four hits for the fourth time in his career.

"We just played a great game tonight," Moustakas said. "Cycle or no cycle, we just played a really good game." ∎

Kansas City Royals pitcher Jeremy Guthrie works against the Oakland Athletics in the first inning. *AP Photo*

18

JUNE 28, 2015 O.CO COLISEUM OAKLAND, CALIFORNIA
KC ROYALS 5 • OAKLAND ATHLETICS 3

ROYALS GET SWEEP OF A'S

Kansas City Royals' Salvador Perez, right, celebrates with teammate Lorenzo Cain after hitting a two-run home run off Oakland Athletics' Edward Mujica in the eighth inning. *AP Photo*

The Kansas City Royals continue to show why they are the team to beat in the American League.

Right-hander Jeremy Guthrie pitched six strong innings, catcher Salvador Perez hit a two-run homer, and the Royals rallied for a 5-3 victory against the Oakland A's on Sunday, sweeping the three-game series at the O.co Coliseum.

The sweep was the reigning AL champion's first against Oakland since Sept. 2-4, 2008, at Kauffman Stadium and the Royals' first at the Coliseum since July 28-30, 2008.

Oakland won five consecutive games before the Royals came to town with their brooms.

"It's huge," Guthrie said of the sweep. "This team has been playing well lately. We got some late runs and were able to win a couple of different ways. It was a big series for us, and hopefully we can carry that momentum down in (Houston) and play another very tough AL West team."

The Royals (44-28) own the American League's best record. They won their fourth straight game, improving to 5-1 on their nine-game road trip and

moving a season-high 16 games over .500.

Guthrie (6-5) allowed two runs on seven hits, walked one and struck out a season-high seven. He struck out the side in the second and sixth innings. In the second inning, he recorded his 1,000th career strikeout, fanning A's first baseman Ike Davis.

"It's 1,000 more than I probably ever thought I'd have 10 years ago," Guthrie said. "It's a great accomplishment to be able to get there and have the endurance to get to that number."

Perez had a milestone day, too. He collected his 500th career hit in the eighth-inning when he homered off A's reliever Edward Mujica.

"Means a lot," said Perez, who drove in three runs and scored twice Sunday. "It's pretty special to me."

A's right-hander Jesse Chavez (4-6) gave up three runs on six hits over 5 2/3 innings, snapping his two-game winning streak. He struck out four and walked two.

The Royals trailed 2-0 entering the sixth inning, but they scored three runs to take the lead and knock Chavez out of the game.

Third baseman Mike Moustakas drilled a leadoff double to right-center and moved to third on first baseman Kendrys Morales' sharp single to right. With one out, Perez hit a slow ground ball that third baseman Max Muncy fielded cleanly on the run, but his throw home was late and off target. Moustakas scored on a fielder's choice, and the runners advanced to second and third on Muncy's error.

Chavez walked left fielder Alex Gordon intentionally, and right fielder Alex Rios hit a sacrifice fly to center as the Royals pulled even.

Second baseman Omar Infante lined an RBI single to right, putting Kansas City ahead 3-2 and ending Chavez's day.

The Royals extended their lead to 5-2 in the eighth. Pinch hitter Lorenzo Cain grounded a leadoff single to center, and Perez crushed Mujica's 3-2, belt-high fastball deep into the left field seats for his 12th home run of the season.

"He left a pitch up and I hit it pretty good," Perez said.

The A's cut Kansas City's lead to 5-3 with a run in the eighth off reliever Kelvin Herrera.■

JULY 27, 2015 • PROGRESSIVE FIELD • CLEVELAND, OHIO

KC ROYALS 9 • CLEVELAND INDIANS 4

ROYALS ROLL OVER INDIANS 9-4

Kansas City Royals First base Eric Hosmer (35) belts a 3-run home run during the first inning. *AP Photo*

The finish may be more important than the start, but sometimes, playing catch-up proves to be too much to handle.

The Kansas City Royals (60-38), the American League's best team, started fast in the first of three straight games against the Cleveland Indians (45-53) at Progressive Field, and never let off the gas as they handed the home team its seventh straight loss in the form of a 9-4 defeat Monday night.

The Royals went to work quickly against Indians rookie pitcher Cody Anderson in the top of the first inning.

With one out, third baseman Mike Moustakas singled a 2-2 offering to left field, and center fielder Lorenzo Cain drew a walk to put two runners on base for clean-up hitter Eric Hosmer. The Royals' veteran first baseman belted the first pitch he saw from Anderson over the wall in center field for a three-run home run.

Then, in the top of the second inning, second baseman Omar Infante blasted a one-out solo home run to left field as the Royals, riding the momentum of their acquisition of ace Johnny Cueto, improved to 15-5 in their last 20 games.

"This is a fun team," manager Ned Yost said. "We do a lot of things well. It's a nice, loose atmosphere. We're playing really good baseball."

At 60-38, the Royals have equaled the best start in franchise history through 98 games. They had the same record in 1976 and 1980.

Already up by a 4-1 count, the Royals continued to pour on the offense against Anderson in the top of the fifth inning.

Shortstop Alcides Escobar doubled to left to start the inning and moved over to third base when Moustakas grounded out to Jason Kipnis at second. Then, Cain drew another walk, and Hosmer smacked an RBI single to right field that drove in Escobar.

Designated hitter Kendrys Morales followed with a double to the wall in deep right-center field, which brought in both Cain and Hosmer and put the Royals in front of the Indians, 7-1.

The Royals increased their advantage to 9-1 with two runs in the top of the seventh inning.

Cain got the rally started with a single to right field, and Hosmer followed with a base hit of his own to right field. Then, Morales singled to center field and drove in Cain. Hosmer came in to score when catcher Salvador Perez lifted a sacrifice fly to right field.

Hosmer, who drove in four runs on the day, said Cueto is joining a team brimming with confidence.

"It's an easy group to get along with," Hosmer said. "We have a lot of fun. When the game starts we play, we give everything we've got. We know he's similar type guy. We're looking forward to having him." ■

Cleveland Indians Second base Jason Kipnis (22) is tagged out at home plate by Kansas City Royals Catcher Salvador Perez (13) trying to score on a fly ball. *AP Photo*

Kansas City Royals' third baseman Mike Moustakas (8) hits a solo home run in the second inning.
AP Photo

SEPTEMBER 24, 2015   KAUFFMAN STADIUM   KANSAS CITY, MISSOURI
KC ROYALS 10 • SEATTLE MARINERS 4

ROYALS CLAIM FIRST DIVISION CROWN IN 30 YEARS

Kansas City Royals' starting pitcher Johnny Cueto (47) tosses a pitch against the Seattle Mariners. *AP Photo*

The wait is over for Kansas City fans.

Behind the booming bat of Mike Moustakas and solid pitching from Johnny Cueto, the Royals thrashed the Seattle Mariners 10-4 Thursday night at Kaufmann Stadium.

The victory over Seattle, coupled with Minnesota's 6-3 loss to Cleveland, wrapped up the AL Central for a Royals team that dominated the division this season, leading by as many as 14 games.

It is the Royals' first division crown since 1985, when they won the AL West en route to their only World Series championship.

The crowd of 32,244 cheered when the Twins'

Kansas City Royals' first baseman Eric Hosmer (35) celebrates after winning the AL Central Division title. *AP Photo*

final score was shown on the scoreboard in the top of the ninth.

"I've felt all along we would win this division. I've got my eyes on a much bigger prize," manager Ned Yost said. "This is the first step of it. Last year we were going tooth-and-nail every game. I just had a real confidence in this group from Day 1 of spring training that we were going to win this division and get back to the playoffs."

Cueto (3-6), acquired in a July 26 trade with Cincinnati, allowed three runs on seven hits in seven innings while striking out five and walking two. He was 0-5 in his previous six starts since an Aug. 15 victory.

"Johnny was awesome," Yost said. "A good changeup, good breaking stuff, kept his fastball down."

Moustakas went 3 for 3 with a home run, three RBIs and three runs. He also walked twice.

"It seemed like it took forever, but we continued to battle," said Lorenzo Cain, who had a two-run single in the sixth to put the Royals ahead for good. "We got down early, but guys stepped up in clutch situations."

Moustakas led off the second with his 21st homer, a career high. He drove in two more runs with a single in the eighth.

Eric Hosmer hit a solo shot to center in the fifth to tie the score at 3. The Royals padded their lead with two more runs in the seventh behind RBIs from Alex Rios and Alcides Escobar.

"It's a huge accomplishment," said Zobrist, who had two doubles and scored three runs. "It hasn't been done here for a long time. There's a lot of guys in this clubhouse I've talked to that have toiled for years to get to this point, to win the division. For them to do it, you can see the kind of sigh of relief, the excitement in the organization."

The Royals have not won a division crown since 1985 when they were in the AL West. The Royals hold a two-game lead over Toronto for the best American League record and homefield advantage.

"We've got to continue to fight," Cain said. "We can't pack it in yet. We'd love to play in front of our home crowd. It's definitely a great feeling to play in front of these guys. They've been supporting us all year long, so we definitely want to win home-field advantage."■

Kansas City Royals' catcher Salvador Perez, left, and third baseman Mike Moustakas get doused with ice water after clinching the Division title.
AP Photo

Play is delayed due to rain in the third inning during Game 1 of the Divisional Series Playoff between the Houston Astros and the Kansas City Royals. *AP Photo*

ER OF MAJOR LEAGUE BASEBALL
OFFICIAL DAILY FANTASY PARTNER OF MAJOR LEAGUE BASEBALL

A fly over concluded the National Anthem prior to Game 1. *AP Photo*

OCTOBER 8, 2015   KAUFFMAN STADIUM   KANSAS CITY, MISSOURI

KC ROYALS 2   •   HOUSTON ASTROS 5

ASTROS JUMP OUT TO SERIES LEAD

Kendrys Morales (25) of the Kansas City Royals celebrates after hitting a home run in the second inning. *AP Photo*

The Houston Astros were able to overcome a nearly hour-long rain delay in Game 1 of the American League Division Series, defeating the reigning American League champion Kansas City Royals 5-2.

Astros manager A.J. Hinch faced a decision after the 49-minute stoppage in the game—whether or not he would keep starter Collin McHugh in the game. Hinch's conventional wisdom when dealing with rain delays is to take out his starting pitcher

if a delay lasts roughly an hour. Ultimately Hinch left McHugh in the game, and it paid off for the visiting Astros.

"We checked in with him a couple times, but he was never really coming out of that game," Hinch said of McHugh, who won 19 games this season. "That wasn't even his best tonight, and he got through a pretty good lineup and battled."

McHugh was able to control much of the game and leave the rest to his bullpen. He pitched 6

Jose Altuve (27) of the Houston Astros is tagged out by Ben Zobrist (18) of the Kansas City Royals. *AP Photo*

innings, surrendering 2 runs on solo home runs by Kendry Morales in the second and fourth innings.

For Royals ace Yordano Ventura, it was a different story. Ventura did not come back after the delay. He gave up three runs on four hits through two innings before Chris Young came on to throw four innings of relief.

George Springer and Colby Rasmus also hit solo home runs to match Morales, but the Astros used the Royals' patented post-season small ball approach to put pressure on Kansas City.

"Winning the first game was key," Astros outfielder Carlos Gomez said. "We did that."

It was an impressive victory for the Astros, who have struggled to win games on the road this season.

"Everyone knows we haven't been playing the best on the road," reliever Tony Sipp said. "To take one in New York and come here, it shows we're a different kind of team."

Houston loaded the bases with no outs in the first inning and struck first with RBI groudouts by Rasmus and Evan Gattis to give the Astros a 2-0 lead in the opening frame.

Jose Altuve delivered an RBI single in the second .

Morales answered in the bottom half, hitting a solo home run down the right-field line.

A steady rain turned into a downpour in the second inning, and lightning halted play as the tarp was pulled onto the field. When the teams were cleared to resume play, Royals manager Ned Yost sent Young to the mound in favor of Ventura.

"It was pushing 60 minutes there," said Yost.

Morales took McHugh deep again in the fourth, becoming the first Royals player to hit two home runs in a postseason game since George Brett made history against the Toronto Blue Jays in the 1985 American League Championship Series.

Unfortunately for Kansas City, Morales was the only Royal batter to solve McHugh.

Luke Gregerson came on in the ninth for the save, and the Royals left facing a critical Game 2.

"It's a five-game series," Royals manager Ned Yost said. "It's not a death sentence to lose Game 1." ■

Alex Gordon (4) of the Kansas City Royals fights off pitches during a heavy rainstorm in the third inning. *AP Photo*

BOX SCORE

	1	2	3	4	5	6	7	8	9	R	H	E
Houston	2	1	0	0	1	0	0	1	0	5	11	0
Kansas City	0	1	0	1	0	0	0	0	0	2	6	0

Astros	AB	R	H	RBI	BB	SO	LOB	AVG.
Altuve 2B	5	1	3	1	0	0	1	.600
Springer RF	4	2	2	1	1	1	2	.500
Correa SS	5	0	1	0	0	2	2	.200
Rasmus LF	3	1	1	2	1	1	2	.333
Gattis DH	4	0	1	1	0	1	2	.250
Gómez PR-DH	0	0	0	0	0	0	0	.000
Valbuena 3B	3	0	0	0	1	3	3	.000
Carter 1B	4	0	1	0	0	2	1	.250
González 1B	0	0	0	0	0	0	0	.000
Castro C	4	0	0	0	0	3	3	.000
Marisnick CF	4	1	2	0	0	1	0	.500
Totals	36	5	11	5	3	14	16	

Royals	AB	R	H	RBI	BB	SO	LOB	AVG.
Escobar SS	4	0	0	0	0	1	2	.000
Zobrist 2B	4	0	2	0	0	0	2	.500
Cain CF	4	0	1	0	0	0	1	.250
Hosmer 1B	4	0	0	0	0	0	3	.000
K. Morales DH	4	2	2	2	0	1	0	.500
Moustakas 3B	3	0	0	0	0	0	0	.000
Pérez C	4	0	0	0	0	1	1	.000
Gordon LF	4	0	1	0	0	0	1	.250
Rios RF	2	0	0	0	1	1	0	.000
Totals	33	2	6	2	1	4	10	

Astros	IP	H	R	ER	BB	SO	HR	ERA
McHugh (W, 1-0)	6.0	4	2	2	1	1	2	3.00
Sipp (H, 1)	1.0	0	0	0	0	0	0	0.00
Harris (H, 1)	0.2	2	0	0	0	1	0	0.00
Pérez (H, 1)	0.1	0	0	0	0	0	0	0.00
Gregerson (S, 1)	1.0	0	0	0	0	2	0	0.00
Totals	9.0	6	2	2	1	4	2	

Royals	IP	H	R	ER	BB	SO	HR	ERA
Ventura (L, 0-1)	2.0	4	3	3	1	2	0	13.50
Young	4.0	3	1	1	2	7	1	2.25
Herrera	1.0	1	0	0	0	2	0	0.00
Madson	1.0	2	1	1	0	3	1	9.00
Hochevar	1.0	1	0	0	0	0	0	0.00
Totals	9.0	11	5	5	3	14	2	

Johnny Cueto (47) of the Kansas City Royals pitches in the fifth inning. *AP Photo*

ROYALS BATTLE BACK TO EVEN SERIES

Kansas City Royals shortstop Alcides Escobar (2) takes a deep breath at third, after hitting a triple.   *AP Photo*

The Kansas City Royals found themselves with their backs against the wall in a crucial Game 2 of the American League Division Series. They used the same brand of baseball that lifted them to last year's World Series to beat the Houston Astros and tie the ALDS at one game apiece.

Ben Zobrist delivered a go-ahead single in the seventh inning to make the score 5-4, and Wade Davis and the blue-collar Royals bullpen held the Astros scoreless in the last two innings to give Kansas City a much-needed victory.

"Just battling," first baseman Eric Hosmer said. "That's what this team does so well."

Down 4-2 in the sixth, Lorenzo Cain hit a rally-sparking double off of Astros starter Scott Kazmir. Manager A.J. Hinch went to Oliver Perez to relieve Kazmir, but Perez would give up back-to-back singles and a walk to load the bases before Josh Fields came on to pitch.

Wade Davis tosses a perfect pitch to first baseman Eric Hosmer (35) picking off Carlos Gomez in the ninth inning of Game 2.
AP Photo

Fields walked Royals catcher Salvador Perez on four straight pitches to knot the game at 4-all.

Alcedes Escobar led off the seventh with a triple against Will Harris, followed by Zobrist's RBI single through the left side to put Kansas City ahead for good.

"We were in position to win that game. Their bullpen did a very good job of shutting us down," Hinch said. "We've got some work to do to win this series. It's going to be a good series. These are two really good teams."

Royals starter Johnny Cueto, who was acquired by Kansas City with October in mind, was shaky from the get-go. Colby Rasmus doubled home a run in the first inning, and George Springer hit a two-run homer in the second in front of an impatient and hostile home crowd.

Perez homered in the bottom of the second to cut Houston's lead to 3-1, but Rasmus hit his third home run of the postseason to put the Astros ahead by 3 runs once again.

Cueto eventually settled in, but with the way Kazmir was pitching, it appeared to be too late. Kazmir allowed just one run in the third but was able to keep Kansas City in check until the sixth inning when the Royals mounted their comeback.

"Just to let it slip away late is kind of a downer," Astros reliever Tony Sipp said. "We had a lead late and let it slip away. We had the momentum going."

With one out in the ninth, Davis walked Preston Tucker, and Carlos Gomez came in as a pinch runner. Davis whipped a throw to Hosmer at first, who made a terrific catch as Gomez dove back to the bag. Gomez was ruled safe, but the call was reviewed and eventually overturned.

"That play that Hos made on the pickoff, I don't know if there's a lot of first basemen that can make that play," Royals manager Ned Yost said. "It was tremendous."▪

BOX SCORE

	1	2	3	4	5	6	7	8	9	R	H	E
Houston	1	2	1	0	0	0	0	0	0	4	8	0
Kansas City	0	1	1	0	0	2	1	0	-	5	11	0

Astros	AB	R	H	RBI	BB	SO	LOB	AVG.
Altuve 2B	5	0	0	0	0	0	3	.300
Springer RF	3	1	1	2	1	1	0	.429
Correa SS	4	0	1	0	0	2	3	.222
Rasmus LF	3	1	2	2	1	0	1	.500
Gattis DH	4	0	1	0	0	0	1	.250
Valbuena 3B	4	0	1	0	0	2	2	.143
Carter 1B	4	1	1	0	0	2	1	.250
Castro C	2	1	0	0	1	0	1	.000
Lowrie PH	1	0	0	0	0	1	0	.000
Marisnick CF	3	0	1	0	0	1	1	.429
Tucker PH	0	0	0	0	1	0	0	.000
Gómez PR	0	0	0	0	0	0	0	.000
Totals	33	4	8	4	4	9	13	

Royals	AB	R	H	RBI	BB	SO	LOB	AVG.
Escobar SS	5	1	2	0	0	1	3	.222
Zobrist 2B	4	0	2	1	0	0	1	.500
Cain CF	4	1	1	0	0	0	2	.250
Hosmer 1B	4	1	1	1	0	0	2	.125
K. Morales DH	4	0	1	0	0	2	1	.375
Moustakas 3B	3	0	0	0	1	0	0	.000
Pérez C	3	1	2	2	1	1	0	.286
Gordon LF	3	0	1	0	1	1	3	.286
Dyson PR-LF	0	0	0	0	0	0	0	.000
Rios RF	3	1	1	0	0	1	4	.200
Orlando	1	0	0	0	0	1	2	.000
Totals	34	5	11	4	3	7	18	

Astros	IP	H	R	ER	BB	SO	HR	ERA
Kazmir	5.1	5	3	3	1	4	1	5.06
Pérez	0.0	2	1	1	1	0	0	27.00
Fields (BS, 1)	0.2	0	0	0	1	2	0	0.00
Harris (L, 0-1)	0.2	2	1	1	0	0	0	6.75
Sipp	0.2	0	0	0	0	0	0	0.00
Neshek	0.2	2	0	0	0	1	0	0.00
Totals	8.0	11	5	5	3	7	1	

Royals	IP	H	R	ER	BB	SO	HR	ERA
Cueto	6.0	7	4	4	3	5	1	6.00
Herrera (W, 1-0)	1.0	1	0	0	0	1	0	0.00
Madson (H, 1)	1.0	0	0	0	0	2	0	4.50
Davis (S, 1)	1.0	0	0	0	1	1	0	0.00
Totals	9.0	8	4	4	4	9	1	

Lorenzo Cain (6) of the Kansas City Royals sprints towards third in the sixth inning. *AP Photo*

Kansas City Royals center fielder Lorenzo Cain (6) touches home plate after hitting a home run during Game 3. *AP Photo*

OCTOBER 11, 2015   MINUTE MAID PARK   HOUSTON, TEXAS
KC ROYALS 2   •   HOUSTON ASTROS 4

ASTROS KEUCHEL TOO MUCH FOR ROYALS

Houston Astros starting pitcher Dallas Keuchel (60) proves too much for the Royals in Game 3.   *AP Photo*

Dallas Keuchel remained perfect at home, and the Houston Astros are one win away from a spot in the American League Championship Series.

Keuchel threw seven innings and propelled the Astros to a 4-2 win over Kansas City. Houston leads the American League Division Series 2-1, and can end the best-of-five series with a win in Game 4.

"The ball in Dallas Keuchel's hand brings an awful lot of confidence to a lot of people. Including me," Astros manager A.J. Hinch said. "And he came up with some excellent pitches."

The attitude of the Kansas City Royals—who have been here before—is quite simple: Win on Monday and force a Game 5 in Kansas City.

"Every game is a must-win," Royals first-baseman Eric Hosmer said. "Obviously, it didn't work out the way we wanted it today. We have to come back and do everything we can to win and take it back to Kansas City."

Royals starter Edinson Volquez has yet to win a postseason game in his career, falling to 0-3 with the loss. He allowed five hits and three runs

Kansas City Royals first baseman Eric Hosmer (35) at the plate during Game 3. *AP Photo*

in five and two-thirds innings of work.

Jason Castro's two run single in the fifth gave the Astros a 2-1 lead after Lorenzo Cain's solo home run in the fourth inning.

Carlos Gomez, who played through a rib muscle strain, added an RBI single in the sixth.

Chris Carter, needing a triple to complete the cycle for the Astros, provided an insurance run for Houston on the first pitch of the seventh inning, launching a solo home run to left-center field.

"You get to this type of scenario and you don't capitalize, you get what happens today," Kansas City manager Ned Yost said.

Volquez didn't allow a hit until the third inning when Carter singled, but ultimately Keuchel proved to be too much for the Royals, mustering only one run off of the Houston ace.

"He threw a great game," Yost said. "I think he should be the Cy Young winner this year. He's been great. He's had a phenomenal year."

Alex Gordon gave the Royals a breath of life in the ninth, hitting a leadoff home run, but Astros closer Luke Gregerson was able to settle in and complete the save.

"We have to stay confident," Cain said. "See what happens tomorrow, come ready to go and give it our all."∎

Kansas City Royals second baseman Ben Zobrist (18) tags Houston Astros first baseman Chris Carter (23). *AP Photo*

BOX SCORE

	1	2	3	4	5	6	7	8	9	R	H	E
Kansas City	0	0	0	1	0	0	0	0	1	2	7	0
Houston	0	0	0	0	2	1	1	0	-	4	8	1

Royals	AB	R	H	RBI	BB	SO	LOB	AVG.
Escobar SS	5	0	2	0	0	0	1	.286
Zobrist 2B	4	0	1	0	0	1	2	.417
Cain CF	4	1	1	1	1	2	3	.250
Hosmer 1B	4	0	0	0	0	3	3	.083
K. Morales DH	3	0	1	0	1	0	0	.364
Moustakas 3B	4	0	1	0	0	1	3	.100
Pérez C	3	0	0	0	1	1	3	.200
Gordon LF	4	1	1	1	0	2	4	.273
Rios RF	3	0	0	0	1	0	0	.125
Totals	34	2	7	2	4	10	19	

Astros	AB	R	H	RBI	BB	SO	LOB	AVG.
Altuve 2B	4	0	0	0	0	1	1	.214
Springer RF	4	1	1	0	0	2	0	.364
Correa SS	4	0	1	0	0	1	1	.231
Rasmus LF	1	0	1	0	3	0	0	.571
Gattis DH	4	0	0	0	0	2	6	.167
Gómez CF	4	0	1	1	0	2	3	.250
Valbuena 3B	1	1	0	0	1	1	1	.125
González PH-3B	1	0	0	0	0	0	2	.000
Lowrie PH-3B	1	0	0	0	0	0	2	.000
Carter 1B	3	2	3	1	0	0	0	.455
Castro C	3	0	1	2	0	1	0	.111
Totals	30	4	8	4	4	10	16	

Royals	IP	H	R	ER	BB	SO	HR	ERA
Vólquez (L, 0-1)	5.2	5	3	3	4	8	0	4.75
Duffy	0.2	1	1	1	0	0	1	13.50
Hochevar	1.2	2	0	0	0	2	0	0.00
Totals	8.0	8	4	4	4	10	1	

Astros	IP	H	R	ER	BB	SO	HR	ERA
Keuchel (W, 1-0)	7.0	5	1	1	3	7	1	1.29
Sipp (H, 2)	0.2	0	0	0	1	2	0	0.00
Gregerson (S, 2)	1.1	2	1	1	0	1	1	3.86
Totals	9.0	7	2	2	4	10	2	

Astros shortstop Carlos Correa (1) jumps high to snag the throw as Alcides Escobar (2) begins his slide. *AP Photo*

OCTOBER 12, 2015   MINUTE MAID PARK   HOUSTON, TEXAS
KC ROYALS 9   •   HOUSTON ASTROS 6

ROYALS STAY ALIVE TO FORCE GAME 5

Kansas City Royals catcher Salvador Perez (13) swings awkwardly at a ball in the third inning. *AP Photo*

Astros shortstop Carlos Correa was having the game of his life. He hit two home runs, added another single, and drove in four runs in Game 4 of the American League Division Series. His team looked well on its way to advancing to the AL Championship Series that would end the Kansas City Royals' season.

A single play changed all of that. Correa mishandled a ground ball in the eighth inning that almost certainly could have turned into a double-play.

The Royals took advantage of the young shortstop's mishap and rallied for five runs in the eighth to take the lead back from the Astros. Kansas City would go on to win 9-6 and even the series at two games apiece, forcing a winner-take-all Game 5 at Kaufmann Stadium.

"We always feel that we're still in games, and we still have a chance," first baseman Eric Hosmer said. "That's the mentality for this whole entire team. It's never quit, and the character we showed today, that's what a championship ballclub does."

The Royals strung together five consecutive

	1	2	3	4	5	6	7	8	9		R
KC	0	2	0	0	0	0	0	4			6
HOU	0	1	1	0	1	0	3				6

Houston Astros left fielder Colby Rasmus (28) looks down as the Royals tie the game in the top of the eighth inning. *AP Photo*

singles off of Houston relief pitchers Will Harris and Tony Sipp. With nobody out, Lorenzo Cain and Hosmer delivered RBI hits to shorten Houston's lead, 6-4.

Kendrys Morales came up with the bases loaded and hit a hard ground ball off of Sipp's glove. The ball skipped twice more, hit off the top of Correa's glove and trickled into center field. Two runs scored to tie the game.

"Just a weird spin on the ball and a tough play," Sipp said. "I'm sure it was tougher than it looked. Game of inches, and I barely missed it."

Alex Gordon added an RBI groundout off of Luke Gregerson later in the eighth to push the Royals ahead for good.

Hosmer supplied some insurance for Kansas City, hitting a two-run bomb in the ninth.

The Royals are no stranger to these kind of come-from-behind victories. Last year, they rallied from a four-run deficit in the eighth inning of the American League wild-card game against the Oakland A's, winning the game in extra innings.

Despite giving up two home runs in the seventh inning, Ryan Madson was able to get the win for the Royals.

Wade Davis threw two scoreless innings for his second save this postseason, while Sipp was credited with the loss.

Kansas City manager Ned Yost believed in his team despite being behind in yet another postseason game.

"You have confidence that sooner or later they're going to put together some hits, they're going to put some runs on the board," said manager Ned Yost, whose Royals will host Game 5 on Wednesday night. "And even though we were down four in the eighth inning, I felt real confident that we were going to make a game out of it. I just felt that the bats were going to come alive, and they really did in the eighth inning. I mean really did."■

Kansas City Royals players celebrate their victory over the Astros to force Game 5. *AP Photo*

BOX SCORE

	1	2	3	4	5	6	7	8	9	R	H	E
Kansas City	0	2	0	0	0	0	0	5	2	9	8	0
Houston	0	1	1	0	1	0	3	0	0	6	9	1

Royals	AB	R	H	RBI	BB	SO	LOB	AVG.
Escobar SS	4	1	1	0	0	2	4	.278
Zobrist 2B	4	2	1	0	1	0	2	.375
Cain CF	5	1	1	1	0	3	2	.235
Hosmer 1B	5	2	2	3	0	1	1	.176
K. Morales DH	4	0	0	1	0	1	1	.267
Dyson PR-DH	1	0	0	0	0	1	0	.000
Moustakas 3B	4	1	1	0	1	1	2	.143
Pérez C	2	1	1	2	0	0	1	.250
Gore PR	0	0	0	0	0	0	0	.000
Butera C	0	0	0	0	1	0	0	.000
Gordon LF	3	0	0	1	1	1	3	.214
Rios RF	3	1	1	0	1	2	1	.182
Orlando PR-RF	0	0	0	0	0	0	0	.000
Totals	35	9	8	8	5	12	17	

Royals	IP	H	R	ER	BB	SO	HR	ERA
Ventura	5.0	4	3	3	3	8	2	7.71
Herrera	1.0	0	1	1	2	3	0	3.00
Madson (W, 1-0)	1.0	4	2	2	0	2	2	9.00
Davis (S, 2)	2.0	1	0	0	0	3	0	0.00
Totals	9.0	9	6	6	5	16	4	

Astros	AB	R	H	RBI	BB	SO	LOB	AVG.
Altuve 2B	4	1	0	0	1	1	0	.167
Springer RF	4	1	0	0	1	4	1	.267
Correa SS	4	2	4	4	0	0	0	.412
Rasmus LF	4	1	2	1	1	2	1	.545
Gattis DH	4	0	1	0	0	1	4	.188
Marisnick PR-DH	0	0	0	0	0	0	0	.429
Tucker PH	1	0	0	0	0	1	1	.000
Gómez CF	5	1	2	1	0	1	1	.333
Valbuena 3B	2	0	0	0	2	0	2	.100
Carter 1B	3	0	0	0	0	2	2	.357
González 1B	1	0	0	0	0	1	2	.000
Castro C	3	0	0	0	0	3	1	.083
Lowrie PH	1	0	0	0	0	0	0	.000
Conger C	0	0	0	0	0	0	0	.000
Totals	36	6	9	6	5	16	15	

Astros	IP	H	R	ER	BB	SO	HR	ERA
McCullers	6.1	2	2	2	2	7	1	2.84
Harris (H, 2)	0.2	4	4	3	0	1	0	18.00
Sipp (L, 0-1; B, 1)	0.1	1	1	0	0	1	0	0.00
Gregerson	0.2	0	0	0	2	1	0	3.00
Fields	1.0	1	2	2	1	2	1	10.80
Totals	9.0	8	9	7	5	12	2	

Kendrys Morales (25) celebrates with Lorenzo Cain (6) of the Kansas City Royals after Morales hit a three run home run during Game 5. *AP Photo*

OCTOBER 14, 2015   KAUFFMAN STADIUM   KANSAS CITY, MISSOURI
KC ROYALS 9   •   HOUSTON ASTROS 6

CUETO SHINES, ROYALS PUNCH TICKET BACK TO ALCS

The Kansas City Royals celebrate after defeating the Houston Astros in Game 5. *AP Photo*

In late July, the Kansas City Royals traded away a number of young prospects to acquire Johnny Cueto from the Cincinatti Reds, who would be counted on in situations like Game 5 of the American League Divisional Series.

With the season on the line, Cueto delivered one of his finest pitching performances to date, throwing eight innings that propelled the Royals to a 7-2 victory over the Houston Astros and a second consecutive AL Championship Series.

Cueto allowed two hits—both in the second inning—before shutting down the next 19 batters.

"I woke up today on the right foot," Cueto said. "As soon as I woke up, I felt something magic, that this was Game 5 and I had to show up for everybody, for this team and the fans."

Salvador Perez (13) and Alex Gordon (4) celebrate after scoring on a double from Alex Rios. *AP Photo*

A single by Evan Gattis followed by a two-run home run by Luis Valbuena in the second were the only blemishes on Cueto's stat line that included eight strikeouts and zero walks. This was the kind of dominating effort the Royals expected when they made the trade for Cueto.

"Johnny Cueto was unbelievable," Royals manager Ned Yost said. "He knew the magnitude of this game. I think we all did. And he came out from the first pitch and had everything going."

Royals closer Wade Davis cruised through he ninth inning, and the celebration in Kansas City was on.

The victory took yet another—albeit slight—comeback, which is becoming all to familiar for Kansas City in the postseason as of late.

The Astros led through four innings before Alex Rios sparked a comeback with a two-run double to take the lead back for the Royals in the fifth. Ben Zorbist and Eric Hosmer each had an RBI to contribute in the win.

"After the homer [Cueto] settled in. He was able to use deception, quick-pitch, slow us down and disrupt our timing," Houston's George Springer said. "He's got electric stuff."

The Royals were able to figure out Collin McHugh this time around, who won Game 1 of the series. McHugh lasted four innings, giving up three earned runs on five hits.

Kendrys Morales added a three-run home run in the eighth inning off Dallas Keuchel to put an exclamation mark on the game and the series. Yet, the game belonged to Cueto, who proved to be a smart investment for the Kansas City Royals.

"Tonight was Cueto's night," Astros manager A.J. Hinch said. "We didn't get a baserunner after the second, is that right? By my book. I thought the crowd got behind him, and he pitches with emotion. He rose to the occasion. This was his night" ∎

BOX SCORE

	1	2	3	4	5	6	7	8	9	R	H	E
Houston	0	2	0	0	0	0	0	0	0	2	2	0
Kansas City	0	0	0	1	3	0	0	3	-	7	8	0

Astros	AB	R	H	RBI	BB	SO	LOB	AVG.
Altuve 2B	4	0	0	0	0	0	0	.136
Springer RF	4	0	0	0	0	2	0	.211
Correa SS	3	0	0	0	0	0	0	.350
Rasmus LF	3	0	0	0	0	3	0	.429
Gómez CF	3	0	0	0	0	1	0	.250
Gattis DH	3	1	1	0	0	1	0	.211
Valbuena 3B	3	1	1	2	0	0	0	.154
Carter 1B	3	0	0	0	0	1	0	.294
Castro C	2	0	0	0	0	0	0	.071
Tucker PH	1	0	0	0	0	1	0	.000
Totals	29	2	2	2	0	9	0	

Royals	AB	R	H	RBI	BB	SO	LOB	AVG.
Escobar SS	3	1	1	0	0	0	1	.286
Zobrist 2B	2	0	0	1	1	1	1	.333
Cain CF	3	2	1	0	1	0	1	.250
Hosmer 1B	4	0	1	1	0	0	2	.190
K. Morales DH	4	1	1	3	0	0	1	.263
Moustakas 3B	4	0	0	0	0	0	1	.111
Pérez C	2	1	1	0	0	0	0	.286
Gordon LF	3	1	1	0	0	0	1	.235
Rios RF	3	1	2	2	0	1	0	.286
Orlando RF	0	0	0	0	0	0	0	.000
Totals	28	7	8	7	2	3	8	

Astros	IP	H	R	ER	BB	SO	HR	ERA
McHugh (L, 1-1)	4.0	5	3	3	1	1	0	4.50
Fiers	1.0	1	1	1	0	0	0	9.00
Sipp	1.2	0	0	0	0	1	0	0.00
Neshek	0.1	0	0	0	0	1	0	0.00
Keuchel	1.0	2	3	3	1	0	1	4.50
Totals	8.0	8	7	7	2	3	1	

Royals	IP	H	R	ER	BB	SO	HR	ERA
Cueto (W, 1-0)	8.0	2	2	2	0	8	1	3.86
Davis	1.0	0	0	0	0	1	0	0.00
Totals	9.0	2	2	2	0	9	1	

▲ Alex Gordon (4) of the Kansas City Royals makes a sliding catch in the sixth inning. *AP Photo*

◄ Salvador Perez, right, gives head coach Ned Yost an ice bath after defeating the Houston Astros in Game 5. *AP Photo*

Ned Yost celebrates with his team following a recent game. *AP Photo*

YOST IS RIGHT MAN FOR THE JOB

Ned Yost is the perfect fit for the Kansas City Royals. Yes, he gets criticized from time to time for some of his in-game moves (or lack thereof), but it is hard to argue with the results as the Royals head back to their second consecutive World Series appearance.

Yost arrived in Kansas City in 2010 with the mandate to develop young talent as he did in Milwaukee. Dayton Moore, the Royals' general manager, worked with Yost in Atlanta. He dismisses the end of Yost's tenure with the Brewers as irrelevant. "There's so much more to managing a baseball team than what's happening on the field," Moore says. When the Royals' losses mounted, Moore didn't flinch. "A lot of people were saying we needed to make a change," he says. "It never crossed my mind."

Moore had spent enough time in the clubhouse to notice how Yost and his charges interacted. Instead of data points to be plugged into an equation, he treated players with sportive affection, like favored nephews. "I love these guys," Yost said in a recent interview. "I really love them. You have to, in order to understand them. And you have to understand them in order to manage them. If you understand their backgrounds, why they are the way they are, you can understand what motivates them."

Like most modern clubhouses, Kansas City's is an eclectic mix. Chris Young is a cerebral Princeton graduate. Lorenzo Cain was raised by his mother in rural Florida and didn't play baseball until high school. Drew Butera's father and Mike Moustakas's uncle were major leaguers. There are Dominicans and Venezuelans, a Puerto Rican, a Nicaraguan, a Cuban and sometimes even a Brazilian. "This is a very culturally diverse team," says Ben Zobrist, a utility player who was traded to Kansas City from Oakland in July. "But these guys for sure feel comfortable with each other. When a clubhouse is that comfortable, it has started with the manager."

To Zobrist, an ideal clubhouse is one where you can't tell whether a team has lost or won four games in a row. That's possible because of the steady, accretive cadence of baseball, a sport in which alternating games of no hits and three hits will win you a batting title. "Most managers don't let you do it," he says. "You pick up clues from the manager. If he's worried, you need to be worried. Here, you have the freedom to think that whatever happened

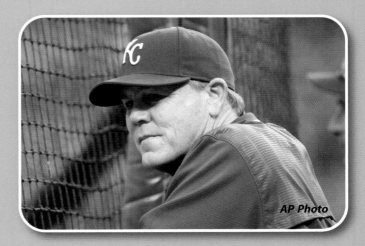

AP Photo

yesterday doesn't matter."

The Royals' success isn't all about intangibles. A decade of high draft picks has paid off with a cadre of homegrown stars. And Moore has constructed a roster of line-drive hitters and fleet fielders tailored to the capacious dimensions of Kansas City's Kauffman Stadium. It's also ideally suited for the economics of playing in the sport's second-smallest metropolitan area: Building a team around outfield defense and middle relief is cheap compared with the marquee expenses of power hitting and starting pitching.

Still, it's telling that castoffs and prospects on downward trajectories have, one after another, righted themselves under Yost. The Royals' burly third baseman, Mike Moustakas, the second pick in the amateur draft, who had been successful at every minor-league level, was struggling last season, his batting average lower than his weight. "I kept hearing: 'Why are you playing him? Why are you playing him?'" Yost says. Moustakas would arrive each day wondering if he'd be dropped from the lineup. Finally, it dawned on him that no matter how badly he performed, Yost wasn't going to remove him. The effect was liberating. His five postseason homers led the team.

"He finds a way to get each of us to believe in what he's doing," Moustakas says. "For me, it really helped to get out there, struggle and learn how to work through failure. It made all the difference." This year, Moustakas was named an American League All-Star. When Yost made the announcement, he beamed like a proud uncle.∎

Kauffman Stadium prior to the start of the ALCS Game 1 between the Toronto Blue Jays and the Kansas City Royals. *AP Photo*

Toronto Blue Jays left fielder Ben Revere (7) leaps to try and stop a home run as a fan tries to catch the ball with his hat.
AP Photo

OCTOBER 16, 2015   KAUFFMAN STADIUM   KANSAS CITY, MISSOURI
KC ROYALS 5 • TORONTO BLUE JAYS 0

VOLQUEZ LEADS ROYALS IN ALCS OPENER

Kansas City Royals starting pitcher Edinson Volquez (36) throws a pitch at the beginning of the ALCS Game 1. *AP Photo*

Edinson Volquez matched teammate Johnny Cueto.

Volquez and three Kansas City Royals relievers combined to shutout the Toronto Blue Jays 5-0 in Game 1 of the American League Championship Series Friday night at Kauffman Stadium.

The Blue Jays, who topped the majors with 891 runs in the regular season — 127 more than any other club — were shut out only five times during the regular season.

Volquez limited the Blue Jays to two singles over six innings, but had to work around four walks. Cueto limited the Houston Astros to two hits over eight innings in the ALDS clincher Wednesday.

"Eddie was superb, had everything going on, had his great fastball, locating well, really good curveball, really nice changeups, on the attack from the first inning on," Royals manager Ned Yost said.

Ben Zobrist (18) gets a base hit. *AP Photo*

Volquez weaved through a treacherous sixth inning, throwing 37 pitches and reaching full counts on four batters. He walked Josh Donaldson to start the inning. He had Jose Bautista down in the count 0-2 and he fouled off the next two pitches. Bautista wound up drawing a walk on nine pitches. That brought up Edwin Encarnacion, who struck out looking.

Chris Colabello lined out to left fielder Alex Gordon on a full-count pitch. Again, Troy Tulowitzki worked the count full before looking at a 95 mile per hour sinker for a called strike.

Volquez walked off the mound with 39,753 fans standing and chanting, "Eddie, Eddie, Eddie."

Kelvin Herrera took the baton in the seventh. He threw nine pitches, all strikes, in retiring the Blue Jays in order, striking out two. Ryan Madson worked around a single and a walk in the eighth and Luke Hochevar finished it up with a hitless ninth.

The Royals opened the scoring with two runs in the third. Gordon started the inning by pulling a Marco Estrada 91 mile per hour fastball into the right-field corner. After one out, shortstop Alcides Escobar hit a ground-ball double to right on an Estrada curveball, scoring Gordon. Escobar, a notorious first-pitch swinger, doubled on the first two Estrada pitches he viewed.

"Always, I swing the first pitch," Escobar said. "When I swing at the first pitch, we're like 40-19. Everyone says just continue to swing the bat."

Center fielder Lorenzo Cain's two-out single brought Escobar home. Cain extended his postseason-hitting streak to 11 games, one shy of the Royals' record held by Amos Otis.

The Royals hiked their lead to 3-0 in the fourth when catcher Salvador Perez homered on Estrada's first offering over the left-center fence after two out.

The Royals padded their lead in the eighth with an Eric Hosmer double scoring Escobar, who was hit by a LaTroy Hawkins pitch to lead off the inning. Hosmer's laser double came within inches of clearing the right-field field fence.

"I got in a hitters' count and was just trying to drive the ball there and get some extra runs in," Hosmer said.

Kendrys Morales' sacrifice fly scored Ben Zobrist, who had reached on an infield stop and stopped at third on Hosmer's double.∎

Alex Gordon (4) pulls a pitch foul during the fourth inning. *AP Photo*

BOX SCORE

	1	2	3	4	5	6	7	8	9	R	H	E
Toronto	0	0	0	0	0	0	0	0	0	0	3	1
Kansas City	0	0	2	1	0	0	0	2	-	5	8	1

Blue Jays	AB	R	H	RBI	BB	SO	LOB	AVG.
Revere LF	4	0	0	0	0	1	2	.000
Donaldson 3B	3	0	1	0	1	0	1	.333
Bautista RF	1	0	0	0	3	1	0	.000
Encarnación DH	3	0	0	0	0	1	3	.000
Smoak PH-DH	1	0	0	0	0	0	2	.000
Colabello 1B	4	0	1	0	0	0	4	.250
Tulowitzki SS	4	0	0	0	0	2	3	.000
Navarro C	4	0	0	0	0	1	0	.000
Pillar CF	3	0	0	0	1	0	1	.000
Goins 2B	3	0	1	0	0	1	1	.333
Totals	30	0	3	0	5	7	17	

Royals	AB	R	H	RBI	BB	SO	LOB	AVG.
Escobar SS	3	2	2	1	0	0	0	.667
Zobrist 2B	4	1	1	0	0	0	2	.250
Cain CF	4	0	1	1	0	1	3	.250
Hosmer 1B	4	0	1	1	0	0	2	.250
K. Morales DH	3	0	1	1	0	2	0	.333
Moustakas 3B	4	0	0	0	0	2	3	.000
Pérez C	3	1	1	1	0	0	0	.333
Gordon LF	3	1	1	0	0	0	0	.333
Rios RF	3	0	0	0	0	2	1	.000
Orlando RF	0	0	0	0	0	0	0	.000
Totals	33	2	6	2	1	4	10	

Blue Jays	IP	H	R	ER	BB	SO	HR	ERA
Estrada (L, 0-1)	5.1	6	3	3	0	6	1	5.06
Loup	0.2	0	0	0	0	0	0	0.00
Lowe	1.0	0	0	0	0	1	0	0.00
Hawkins	1.0	2	2	2	0	0	0	18.00
Totals	8.0	8	5	5	0	7	1	

Royals	IP	H	R	ER	BB	SO	HR	ERA
Vólquez (W, 1-0)	6.0	2	0	0	4	5	0	0.00
Herrera (H, 1)	1.0	0	0	0	0	2	0	0.00
Madson (H, 1)	1.0	1	0	0	1	0	0	0.00
Hochevar	1.0	0	0	0	0	0	0	0.00
Totals	9.0	3	0	0	5	7	0	

OCTOBER 17, 2015   KAUFFMAN STADIUM   KANSAS CITY, MISSOURI
KC ROYALS 6 • TORONTO BLUE JAYS 3

ROYALS RALLY LATE TO KNOCK OFF BLUE JAYS

Kansas City Royals shortstop Alcides Escobar (2) dives for a catch. *AP Photo*

After David Price dominated for six scoreless innings, allowing one hit, the Kansas City Royals' dormant offense woke up Saturday.

Alex Gordon hit a go-ahead double in a five-run seventh as the Royals batted around and rallied for a 6-3 victory over the Toronto Blue Jays on Saturday to take a 2-0 lead in the American League Championship Series.

It should not come as a surprise that the Royals' rallied late. They were down four runs in the eighth inning in the 2014 wild-card game to Oakland, but rallied to win. They trailed at Houston by four runs in the eighth inning Monday and on the verge of being eliminated, but came back to win.

So a five-run seventh inning off Price should not be a shocker.

"It was crazy, but I've seen it before," said winning pitcher Danny Duffy. "Never doubt our guys."

Kansas City Royals first baseman Eric Hosmer (35) slides across home plate to score in the eighth inning. *AP Photo*

Price allowed only a leadoff single on his first pitch of the game to shortstop Alcides Escobar until the seventh.

Price retired the next 18 batters, a Blue Jays' record for consecutive batters retired in a postseason game, while striking out seven, including the side in the sixth.

In the seventh, Price, who is winless in seven career postseason starts, and the Blue Jays became unraveled.

The inning began with second baseman Ben Zobrist hitting a flare to shallow right that dropped between second baseman Ryan Goins and right fielder Jose Bautista for a single.

Lorenzo Cain followed with a crisp single to right, extending his postseason hitting streak to 11 games, tying a club record.

First baseman Eric Hosmer singled to center, bringing home Zobrist with the first Kansas City run and advancing Cain to third. Cain scored on designated hitter Kendrys Morales' ground out.

"This place is magical," Hosmer said. "When Zobrist gets that first knock and Lo Cain follows it up, you know you've got something brewing. Keeping the line moving and we just got it done."

Third baseman Mike Moustakas snapped an 0-for-13 skid with a RBI single to tie it and advanced to second on the throw home.

After Price struck out catcher Salvador Perez, left fielder Gordon worked the count full before doubling to right-center to drive in Moustakas and put the Royals in front 4-3.

Gordon turned on Price's 96 mph fastball, which was his 30th and final pitch of the inning. He had not thrown more than 14 pitches in any of the first six innings.

Aaron Sanchez replaced Price and promptly gave up a run-producing single to right fielder Alex Rios.

Moustakas' two-out eighth inning single scored Hosmer with an insurance run as Kansas City won its nine straight ALCS contest, one shy of the record held by the Baltimore Orioles (1969-73).

The Blue Jays scored two runs in the sixth, when designated hitter Edwin Encarnacion's single drove in third baseman Josh Donaldson with the first run.

Kansas City Royals left fielder Alex Gordon (4) celebrates on 2nd base after hitting a double. *AP Photo*

BOX SCORE

	1	2	3	4	5	6	7	8	9		R	H	E
Toronto	0	0	1	0	0	2	0	0	0		3	10	0
Kansas City	0	0	0	0	0	0	5	1	-		6	8	0

Blue Jays	AB	R	H	RBI	BB	SO	LOB	AVG.
Revere LF	5	0	0	0	0	2	3	.000
Donaldson 3B	5	1	1	0	0	2	3	.250
Bautista RF	4	1	0	0	1	1	3	.000
Encarnación DH	4	0	2	1	0	2	0	.286
Colabello 1B	4	0	2	0	0	1	2	.375
Tulowitzki SS	4	0	2	1	0	1	3	.250
Martin C	3	0	0	0	1	1	4	.000
Pillar CF	4	1	2	0	0	0	3	.286
Goins 2B	3	0	1	1	0	1	3	.333
Pennington PH	0	0	0	0	1	0	0	.000
Totals	36	3	10	3	3	11	24	

Royals	AB	R	H	RBI	BB	SO	LOB	AVG.
Escobar SS	4	0	1	0	0	1	1	.429
Zobrist 2B	4	1	1	0	0	1	1	.250
Cain CF	3	1	1	0	1	0	1	.286
Hosmer 1B	3	2	1	1	1	2	1	.286
K. Morales DH	3	0	0	1	1	1	1	.167
Moustakas 3B	4	1	2	2	0	0	0	.250
Pérez C	4	0	0	0	0	1	3	.143
Gordon LF	3	1	1	1	0	1	0	.333
Ríos RF	3	0	1	1	0	1	0	.167
Orlando PR-RF	0	0	0	0	0	0	0	.000
Totals	31	6	8	6	3	8	8	

Blue Jays	IP	H	R	ER	BB	SO	HR	ERA
Price (L, 0-1)	6.2	6	5	5	0	8	0	6.75
Sanchez	0.2	1	0	0	1	0	0	0.00
Loup	0.1	1	1	1	2	0	0	9.00
Lowe	0.1	0	0	0	0	0	0	0.00
Totals	8.0	8	6	6	3	8	0	

Royals	IP	H	R	ER	BB	SO	HR	ERA
Ventura	5.1	8	3	3	2	6	0	5.06
Hochevar	0.2	0	0	0	0	0	0	0.00
Duffy (W, 1-0)	1.0	0	0	0	0	1	0	0.00
Herrera (H, 2)	1.0	1	0	0	0	2	0	0.00
Davis (S, 1)	1.0	1	0	0	1	2	0	0.00
Totals	9.0	3	0	0	5	7	0	

Bautista, who had walked, scored on shortstop Troy Tulowitzki's double.

Royals starter Yordano Ventura failed to survive the inning. Luke Hochevar was summoned with one out and the bases full, and retired Kevin Pillar and Goins on five pitches, keeping the ball in the infield.

Right-hander Wade Davis yielded a single and a walk to begin the ninth, but posted his third postseason save. Duffy picked up the victory, pitching a spotless seventh inning.■

Kansas City Royals Starting pitcher
Johnny Cueto (47) points to the crowd
during the ALCS Game 3. *AP Photo*

OCTOBER 19, 2015   ROGERS CENTRE   TORONTO, ONTARIO
KC ROYALS 8 • TORONTO BLUE JAYS 11

BLUE JAYS BATS COME ALIVE IN 11-8 WIN

Kansas City Royals Kendrys Morales (25) hits a two-run homer in the ninth inning.   *AP Photo*

There was nothing wrong with the Toronto Blue Jays that a return home could not fix. After being held to three runs while losing the first two games of the American League Championship Series to the Royals in Kansas City, the Blue Jays cranked three home runs Monday and held on for an 11-8 victory in Game 3.

The Royals, who scored four runs in the ninth to make the game close, lead the best-of-seven series 2-1.

Shortstop Troy Tulowitzki hit a three-run homer in the third inning. Third baseman Josh Donaldson added a two-run blast in the third, and second baseman Ryan Goins hit solo shot in the fifth and also played superbly in the field.

Royals designated hitter Kendrys Morales capped a three-hit game with a two-run homer in the ninth. Kansas City shortstop Alcides Escobar had four hits, including a triple, and second baseman Ben Zobrist had three doubles.

Toronto right-hander Marcus Stroman (1-0) picked up his first win in the postseason, allowing

The Royals Ben Zobrist (18) drills a double in the third inning. *AP Photo*

four runs, 11 hits and one walk in 6 1/3 innings.

Royals right-hander Johnny Cueto (1-1) did not retire a batter in Toronto's six-run third. He left after two-plus innings, charged with eight runs on six hits, four walks and a hit batter.

"He couldn't command the ball down," Kansas City manager Ned Yost said. "He just really struggled with his command."

Right-hander Kris Medlen replaced Cueto and allowed two runs on three hits, two of them solo homers, in five innings. Yost said it saved his bullpen.

"Very, very crucial," Yost said. "It was a great job by Kris Medlen."

The Royals scored once in the first after Blue Jays right fielder Jose Bautista misplayed a leadoff hit by Escobar into a triple. Escobar scored on Zobrist's groundout to second.

Toronto replied with three runs in the second.

Tulowitzki singled with one out, and catcher Russell Martin was hit by a pitch. Center fielder Kevin Pillar, who made a sensational catch in the first, forced Martin at second with a grounder to shortstop and stole second uncontested.

Goins hit a two-run single to left, left fielder Ben Revere walked, and Donaldson hit an RBI single.

The Royals cut the lead to 3-2 in the third. Zobrist led off with a double, took third on center fielder Lorenzo Cain's infield single and scored on first baseman Eric Hosmer's grounder to first.

Tulowitzki's second three-run homer of the postseason keyed Toronto's six-run third.

The Royals scored twice in the fifth, trimming the lead to 9-4. Escobar led off with a single, took third on Zobrist's double and scored on a wild pitch. Morales walked and scored on a single by third baseman Mike Moustakas.

Goins homered with two outs in the fifth.

The Blue Jays scored a run in the eighth against left-hander Franklin Morales on Bautista's RBI single.

Blue Jays right-hander Liam Hendriks got only one out, a sacrifice fly by Cain in the ninth, allowing three runs and three hits, including an RBI single by Hosmer.

Right-hander Roberto Osuna allowed the homer by Morales before finishing the game.

"It's always tough when you dig a hole like that." Moustakas said. "Again, this team never quits, never gives up. We showed it again tonight, we just came up a little short."∎

BOX SCORE

	1	2	3	4	5	6	7	8	9	R	H	E
Kansas City	1	0	1	0	2	0	0	0	4	8	15	0
Toronto	0	3	6	0	1	0	0	1	-	11	11	0

Royals	AB	R	H	RBI	BB	SO	LOB	AVG.
Escobar SS	5	3	4	0	0	0	0	.583
Zobrist 2B	5	3	3	1	0	0	1	.385
Cain CF	4	0	1	1	0	0	2	.273
Hosmer 1B	5	1	2	2	0	1	2	.333
K. Morales DH	4	1	3	2	1	0	1	.400
Moustakas 3B	5	0	1	1	0	0	4	.231
Pérez C	5	0	0	0	0	0	3	.083
Gordon LF	4	0	1	0	0	1	0	.300
Rios RF	4	0	0	0	0	0	2	.100
Totals	41	8	15	7	1	2	15	

Blue Jays	AB	R	H	RBI	BB	SO	LOB	AVG.
Revere LF	4	1	1	0	1	0	1	.077
Donaldson 3B	4	1	2	3	1	1	0	.333
Bautista RF	3	0	1	1	2	1	2	.125
Encarnación DH	5	1	2	0	0	2	4	.333
Colabello 1B	3	1	0	0	1	0	2	.273
Smoak 1B	1	0	0	0	0	0	2	.000
Tulowitzki SS	4	2	2	3	0	2	0	.333
Pennington 2B	0	0	0	0	0	0	0	.000
Martin C	2	1	0	0	1	2	0	.000
Pillar CF	4	2	1	1	0	0	2	.273
Goins 2B-SS	4	2	2	3	0	1	1	.400
Totals	34	11	11	11	6	9	14	

Royals	IP	H	R	ER	BB	SO	HR	ERA
Cueto (L, 0-1)	2.0	6	8	8	4	2	1	36.00
Medlen	5.0	3	2	2	1	6	2	3.60
F. Morales	1.0	2	1	1	1	1	0	9.00
Totals	8.0	11	11	11	6	9	3	

Blue Jays	IP	H	R	ER	BB	SO	HR	ERA
Stroman (W, 1-0)	6.1	11	4	4	1	1	0	5.68
Sanchez	0.2	0	0	0	0	0	0	0.00
Lowe	1.0	0	0	0	0	1	0	0.00
Hendriks	0.1	3	3	3	0	0	0	81.00
Osuna	0.2	1	1	1	0	0	1	13.50
Totals	9.0	15	8	8	1	2	1	

Blue Jays infielder Ryan Goins (17) avoids the slide of Alex Rios (15) at second base. *AP Photo*

OCTOBER 20, 2015   ROGERS CENTRE   TORONTO, ONTARIO
KC ROYALS 14 • TORONTO BLUE JAYS 2

ROYALS ROUT JAYS TO TAKE 3-1 SERIES LEAD

Starting pitcher R.A. Dickey (43) pleads with home plate umpire Hunter Wendelstedt after tagging Lorenzo Cain (6) at home plate.
AP Photo

The Kansas City Royals put a 15-hit barrage on the Toronto Blue Jays for the second game in a row Tuesday.

This time they won, 14-2, to take a three-games-to-one lead in the best-of-seven American League Championship Series.

Kansas City could clinch a World Series berth on Wednesday at Rogers Centre.

"We feel good, we like the way we're playing right now," Royals manager Ned Yost said. "Our offense has been really, really good."

Second baseman Ben Zobrist hit a two-run homer in the first inning, and right fielder Alex Rios added a solo shot in the second to give the Royals an early lead against Blue Jays right-hander R.A. Dickey.

The Royals also had 15 hits in Game 3 on Monday, but their late rally fell short and they lost 11-8.

This time they scored five runs (four earned) on four hits and two walks in 1 2/3 innings to chase Dickey (0-1).

Kansas City put the game away with a four-run seventh and added three in the eighth and two in the ninth.

"There's no doubt it's a big challenge," Blue Jays manager John Gibbons said. "It's a do-or-die game Wednesday. I think these guys will let this one go, and they'll show up to play tomorrow."

Gibbons brought in infielder Cliff Pennington to pitch with two outs in the ninth. Pennington allowed a single to right fielder Paulo Orlando and a two-run single by shortstop Alcides Escobar, who had four RBIs.

Royals center fielder Lorenzo Cain went 2-for-3 with two walks and three RBIs to extend his team-record postseason hitting streak to 13 games. Rios finished with three hits.

Kansas City right-hander Chris Young did not stay around long enough to earn the win.

He was lifted for right-hander Luke Hochevar (1-0) with a 5-2 lead and two outs in the fifth after giving up a single to left fielder Ben Revere.

Hochevar ended the inning on a foulout to first by third baseman Josh Donaldson.

Young allowed two runs, three hits and two walks and struck out four.

"Chris Young threw the ball great," Yost said. "We got to the fifth there and my mindset was with Donaldson, (right fielder Jose) Bautista, those guys, I really didn't want them seeing Chris for the third time."

The Royals pounced on Dickey for four first-inning runs, two on a home run by Zobrist after Escobar led off with a bunt single.

The knuckleballer walked Cain, who stole second, took third on a single by first baseman Eric Hosmer and scored on a passed ball. A groundout moved Hosmer to third, and he scored on a sacrifice fly by third baseman Mike Moustakas.

Rios' homer with one out in the second increased the lead to 5-0.

Lorenzo Cain (6) and Jarrod Dyson (1) celebrate after winning Game 4. *AP Photo*

"We were really focused on being productive collectively," said Rios, a former Blue Jay. "And I guess we're doing a pretty good job of doing it. Defensively, we've been good. Offensively, we've been even better, so that's what we've been focusing on."■

Alex Rios (15) drills a one-out home run in the second inning. *AP Photo*

BOX SCORE

	1	2	3	4	5	6	7	8	9	R	H	E
Kansas City	4	1	0	0	0	0	4	3	2	14	15	0
Toronto	0	0	2	0	0	0	0	0	0	2	7	0

Royals	AB	R	H	RBI	BB	SO	LOB	AVG.
Escobar SS	3	1	2	4	0	0	0	.600
Zobrist 2B	5	2	2	2	1	0	3	.389
Cain CF	3	1	2	3	2	1	0	.357
Dyson CF	0	0	0	0	0	0	0	.000
Hosmer 1B	4	1	1	1	0	2	2	.313
K. Morales DH	5	1	1	0	0	0	2	.333
Moustakas 3B	4	0	0	1	0	1	1	.176
Pérez C	3	2	1	0	1	1	0	.133
Butera C	1	0	0	0	0	0	1	.000
Gordon LF	3	3	1	0	1	0	0	.308
Rios RF	3	1	3	1	0	0	0	.308
Orlando PR-RF	2	2	2	0	0	0	0	1.000
Totals	36	14	15	12	5	5	9	

Blue Jays	AB	R	H	RBI	BB	SO	LOB	AVG.
Revere LF	3	1	2	0	1	1	0	.188
Donaldson 3B	3	0	1	1	1	0	2	.333
Bautista RF	4	0	1	0	2	3	3	.167
Encarnación DH	4	0	0	0	0	1	4	.250
Colabello 1B	4	0	0	0	0	0	0	.200
Tulowitzki SS	3	0	1	0	0	0	0	.333
Pompey PH	1	0	1	0	0	0	0	1.000
Martin C	3	0	0	0	0	1	1	.000
Carrera PH	1	0	0	0	0	0	0	.000
Pillar CF	4	0	0	0	0	2	2	.200
Goins 2B	3	1	1	0	0	1	1	.385
Totals	33	2	7	2	2	8	14	

Royals	IP	H	R	ER	BB	SO	HR	ERA
Young	4.2	3	2	2	2	4	0	3.86
Hochevar (W, 1-0)	1.1	1	0	0	0	0	0	0.00
Madson	1.0	1	0	0	0	2	0	0.00
Herrera	1.0	1	0	0	0	1	0	0.00
F. Morales	1.0	1	0	0	0	1	0	4.50
Totals	9.0	7	2	2	2	8	0	

Blue Jays	IP	H	R	ER	BB	SO	HR	ERA
Dickey (L, 0-1)	1.2	4	5	4	2	1	2	21.60
Hendriks	4.1	1	0	0	0	2	0	5.79
Hawkins	0.0	2	3	3	1	0	0	45.00
Tepera	1.2	5	4	4	2	0	0	21.60
Lowe	1.0	1	2	2	0	2	0	5.40
Pennington	0.1	2	0	0	0	0	0	0.00
Totals	9.0	15	14	13	5	5	2	

Toronto Blue Jays starting pitcher Marco Estrada is poised on the mound in the first inning of Game 5. *AP Photo*

OCTOBER 21, 2015   ROGERS CENTRE   TORONTO, ONTARIO
KC ROYALS 1   •   TORONTO BLUE JAYS 7

ESTRADA KEEPS BLUE JAYS HOPES ALIVE

Kansas City Royals catcher Salvador Perez (13) hits a home run in the eighth inning. *AP Photo*

Marco Estrada and his magical changeup gave the Kansas City Royals more than they could handle Wednesday.

At the same time, the right-hander gave the Toronto Blue Jays everything they needed.

He allowed one run, three hits and one walk in 7 2/3 innings, shortstop Troy Tulowitzki had three RBIs and the Blue Jays avoided elimination with a 7-1 victory over the Royals in Game 5 of the American League Championship Series.

The Royals lead the best-of-seven series 3-2, with Game 6 scheduled for Friday at Kauffman Stadium.

"We've seen him pitch like that all year," Blue Jays manager John Gibbons said of Estrada. "He really rose to the occasion."

Estrada (2-1) faced one batter above the minimum before Royals catcher Salvador Perez homered to right with two outs in the eighth inning.

When left fielder Alex Gordon followed with a single, right-hander Aaron Sanchez replaced Estrada. Right fielder Alex Rios singled and shortstop Alcides Escobar flied to right to end the inning.

Tulowitzki doubled with the bases loaded against right-handed reliever Kelvin Herrera for the only hit in a four-run sixth inning to break the game open for Toronto.

Royals right-hander Edinson Volquez (1-2) allowed five runs, three hits and four walks and hit a batter in five-plus innings.

It was a reversal from Game 1 of the ALCS won 5-0 by the Royals when Volquez outpitched Estrada, who said he had trouble with fastball command during that start.

"Today, he was absolutely dynamite, he didn't miss spots," Royals manager Ned Yost said. "His changeup was fantastic."

First baseman Chris Colabello homered with one out in the second to give the Blue Jays a 1-0 lead. It was his second postseason homer.

Estrada retired the first nine hitters before Escobar led off the fourth with a single, but he was erased when second baseman Ben Zobrist grounded into a double play.

Left fielder Ben Revere led off the Toronto sixth with a walk and third baseman Josh Donaldson was hit by a pitch. Right fielder Jose Bautista fouled off four 97 mph fastballs on a full count before walking to load the bases, a close call that the Royals questioned.

"I thought the pitch to Bautista was definitely a strike," Yost said. "I thought we had a chance on him swinging, but we couldn't get anybody's attention on it."

Designated hitter Edwin Encarnacion walked on a full count to force in a run and give Toronto a 2-0 lead.

"Probably could have gone either way; we just didn't get the call there," Yost said.

Herrera replaced Volquez and struck out Colabello before Tulowitzki cleared the bases with

Alcides Escobar (2) throws over a sliding Edwin Encarnacion. *AP Photo*

a double to center and Toronto led 5-0.

"They have home-field advantage," Tulowitzki said. "Our backs are going to be against the wall. We've got to win two games. ... It's possible." ∎

Lorenzo Cain (6) reacts to Home Plate Umpire Dan Iassogna telling him that he is out. *AP Photo*

BOX SCORE

	1	2	3	4	5	6	7	8	9	R	H	E
Kansas City	0	0	0	0	0	0	0	1	0	1	4	0
Toronto	0	1	0	0	0	4	1	1	-	7	8	0

Royals	AB	R	H	RBI	BB	SO	LOB	AVG.
Escobar SS	4	0	1	0	0	0	2	.526
Zobrist 2B	4	0	0	0	0	1	1	.318
Cain CF	3	0	0	0	1	1	0	.294
Hosmer 1B	4	0	0	0	0	0	1	.250
K. Morales DH	3	0	0	0	0	1	0	.278
Moustakas 3B	3	0	0	0	0	1	0	.150
Pérez C	3	1	1	1	0	0	0	.167
Gordon LF	3	0	1	0	0	1	0	.313
Rios RF	3	0	1	0	0	0	0	.313
Totals	30	1	4	1	1	5	4	

Blue Jays	AB	R	H	RBI	BB	SO	LOB	AVG.
Revere LF	3	1	0	0	1	1	0	.158
Donaldson 3B	3	2	1	0	0	1	0	.333
Bautista RF	3	1	2	1	1	0	0	.267
Encarnación DH	3	1	0	1	1	1	2	.211
Colabello 1B	4	1	1	1	0	2	4	.211
Smoak 1B	0	0	0	0	0	0	0	.000
Tulowitzki SS	4	1	2	3	0	0	0	.368
Navarro C	3	0	0	0	1	3	2	.000
Pillar CF	4	0	2	1	0	1	2	.263
Goins 2B	3	0	0	0	0	1	1	.313
Totals	30	7	8	7	4	10	11	

Royals	IP	H	R	ER	BB	SO	HR	ERA
Vólquez (L, 1-1)	5.0	3	5	5	4	2	1	4.09
Herrera	1.0	1	0	0	0	3	0	0.00
Duffy	2.0	4	2	2	0	5	0	6.00
Totals	9.0	7	2	2	2	8	0	

Blue Jays	IP	H	R	ER	BB	SO	HR	ERA
Estrada (W, 1-1)	7.2	3	1	1	1	5	1	2.77
Sanchez	0.1	1	0	0	0	0	0	0.00
Osuna	1.0	0	0	0	0	0	0	5.40
Totals	9.0	4	1	1	1	5	1	

Kendrys Morales (25) celebrates after Lorenzo Cain (6) scores to give the Royals the lead.
AP Photo

OCTOBER 23, 2015   KAUFFMAN STADIUM   KANSAS CITY, MISSOURI
KC ROYALS 4 • TORONTO BLUE JAYS 3

ROYALS PUNCH TICKET TO WORLD SERIES!

Kansas City Royals second baseman Ben Zobrist (18) crosses the plate after a home run. *AP Photo*

The Kansas City Royals are returning to the World Series for the second straight season after Lorenzo Cain scored from first base on a single on a gutsy call by third base coach Mike Jirschele.

Cain, who was running hard all the way, scored on Eric Hosmer's single in the bottom of the eighth in Game 6 of the American League Championship Series, and that was the difference as the Kansas City Royals defeated the Toronto Blue Jays 4-3 Saturday night.

The Royals, who lost to the San Francisco Giants in seven games in the 2014 World Series, will play the New York Mets, beginning Tuesday at Kansas City.

"From the first day of spring training, we expected to be here," Royals manager Ned Yost said.

Cain led off the inning with an eight-pitch walk from 20-year-old right-handed closer Roberto Osuna. Hosmer pulled a 2-2 pitch into right field. Jose Bautista threw to second base, instead of throwing the ball home.

"I had a feeling Bautista was going to come up and throw to second base," Jirschele said. "He's been

Mike Moustakas (8) high fives teammate Eric Hosmer (35) after hitting a home run. *AP Photo*

doing it. As soon I saw him release the ball to second, I had Lorenzo coming in. I knew we were going to take a shot at it.

"With Lorenzo running, it was going to take a perfect throw to second and a perfect throw to home and you're going to take your chances on that."

Shortstop Troy Tulowitzki's relay throw was up the line.

Hosmer said the hit ranks "right up there" as the biggest of his career."

Wade Davis gave up a single, a walk and allowed the Blue Jays to steal three bases in the ninth, but did not allow a run.

The Royals had to overcome two Bautista home runs.

Kansas City took a 3-1 lead into the eighth when Bautista homered with Ben Revere on base. Bautista yanked a Ryan Madson 96 mph fastball into the left field seats.

Bautista silenced the sold out Kauffman Stadium crowd of 40,494 that had been booing his every plate-appearance. He also homered in the fourth.

Royals right-hander Yordano Ventura was pulled with one out in the sixth after yielding a double to Edwin Encarnacion. Ventura allowed one run on four hits in 5 1/3 innings, striking out five and walking two.

Kelvin Herrera replaced Ventura and retired all five batters he faced, striking out two, before turning over a two-run lead to Madson in the eighth that he failed to keep for three hitters.

Moustakas led off the seventh with a splintered-bat single to center. Catcher Salvador Perez drove a David Price pitch to the left-field bullpen fence, but Ben Revere made a spectacular leaping grab to rob him of extra-bases. Moustakas advanced to third on left fielder Alex Gordon's ground out.

Price did not finish the inning as rookie right-hander Aaron Sanchez was brought in to face Alex Rios with two out. Rios laced a single to left, scoring Moustakas.

While the Blue Jays topped the majors with 232 home runs during the regular season, the Royals used the long ball to grab an early 2-0 lead.

Second baseman Ben Zobrist punched a David Price 91 mph cutter out to left on a 1-1 count in the first inning for his second home run in this ALCS.

In the second inning, Moustakas belted a Price changeup over the right-field fence. Blue Jays manager John Gibbons requested a review, though, claiming a fan in the first row reached over the wall. After a 107-second delay, the homer stood.∎

Kansas City Royals first baseman Eric Hosmer (35) celebrates after making the final out to advance to the World Series.
AP Photo

BOX SCORE

	1	2	3	4	5	6	7	8	9	R	H	E
Toronto	0	0	0	1	0	0	0	2	0	3	7	0
Kansas City	1	1	0	0	0	0	0	1	1	-	4	9	0

Blue Jays	AB	R	H	RBI	BB	SO	LOB	AVG.
Revere LF	5	1	2	0	0	2	4	.208
Donaldson 3B	5	0	0	0	0	2	6	.261
Bautista RF	4	2	2	3	0	0	1	.316
Encarnación DH	3	0	1	0	1	0	1	.227
Colabello 1B	4	0	1	0	0	1	2	.217
Tulowitzki SS	4	0	0	0	0	2	3	.304
Martin C	3	0	1	0	1	1	0	.091
Pompey PR	0	0	0	0	0	0	0	1.000
Pillar CF	2	0	0	0	2	0	0	.238
Goins 2B	3	0	0	0	0	2	2	.263
Navarro PH	1	0	0	0	0	1	2	.000
Totals	34	3	7	3	4	11	21	

Royals	AB	R	H	RBI	BB	SO	LOB	AVG.
Escobar SS	4	0	1	0	0	1	1	.478
Zobrist 2B	3	1	1	1	1	0	3	.320
Cain CF	3	1	1	0	1	0	0	.300
Hosmer 1B	4	0	1	1	0	1	2	.250
K. Morales DH	4	0	1	0	0	1	0	.273
Gore PR-DH	0	0	0	0	0	0	0	.000
Moustakas 3B	4	2	2	1	0	1	2	.208
Pérez C	4	0	0	0	0	2	3	.136
Gordon LF	3	0	0	0	0	2	1	.263
Rios RF	3	0	2	1	0	0	0	.368
Orlando PR-RF	0	0	0	0	0	0	0	1.000
Totals	32	4	9	4	2	8	12	

Blue Jays	IP	H	R	ER	BB	SO	HR	ERA
Price	6.2	5	3	3	1	8	2	5.40
Sanchez	0.1	2	0	0	0	0	0	0.00
Osuna (L, 0-1)	1.0	2	1	1	1	0	0	6.75
Totals	8.0	9	4	4	2	8	2	

Royals	IP	H	R	ER	BB	SO	HR	ERA
Ventura	5.1	4	1	1	2	5	1	3.38
Herrera (H, 3)	1.2	0	0	0	0	2	0	0.00
Madson (B, 1)	0.1	2	2	2	1	1	1	7.71
Davis (W, 1-0)	1.2	1	0	0	1	3	0	0.00
Totals	9.0	7	3	3	4	11	2	

The Kansas City Royals celebrate after defeating the Blue Jays 4-3 to advance to the World Series.
AP Photo

Alcides Escobar with one of his 11 hits in the ALCS.
AP Photo

ALCS MVP: ALCIDES ESCOBAR

Alcides Escobar caused the Toronto Blue Jays all kinds of trouble from the very first pitch. In just about every game of the AL Championship Series.

The leadoff hitter and defensive dynamo was voted MVP of the ALCS following a 4-3 victory in Game 6 that put Kansas City in its second straight World Series.

Escobar set a postseason record by getting a leadoff hit in the first four games of a series — he scored in two of those games. And he wound up going 11 for 23 against the Blue Jays, joining Dustin Pedroia of the Boston Red Sox as the only hitters to have at least 10 hits and five RBIs from the leadoff spot in LCS history.

Not bad for a career .262 hitter known primarily for his defense.

"He's such a talented player," Royals manager Ned Yost said. "But with the grind of a 162-game season, there are little periods where his focus will tend to waver a little bit. But during the playoffs, he just locks in. And when he's focused, he's as good as any player in the league."

Escobar followed teammate Lorenzo Cain in becoming the second straight Royal to earn ALCS MVP honors. Both were part of the 2010 trade that sent pitcher Zack Greinke to the Milwaukee Brewers — a deal that helped set up Kansas City's run of success.

Despite a lousy on-base percentage, and advance metrics that run against conventional wisdom, Escobar has flourished since returning to the Royals' leadoff spot in late September.

His penchant for swinging at the first pitch suddenly made Yost look like a genius when he opened Game 1 with a first-pitch double off Marco Estrada. He singled again the next night in his first at-bat, and tripled under the glove of Jose Bautista leading off Game 3.

Then, he showed his speed by leading off the Royals' rout in Game 4 with a surprise bunt base hit off knuckleballer R.A. Dickey, eventually jogging home on Ben Zobrist's home run.

In all, Escobar saw six pitches in those first four at-bats.

"I want to go to home plate and be aggressive, trying to swing at a strike," he explained earlier in the series. "And I'm doing really good right now. Continue to be the same guy."

AP Photo

Escobar grounded out on the first pitch from Estrada in Game 5, and in his first at-bat against David Price in Game 6. But he extended his postseason hit streak to 10 games with a single in the seventh, and seemed to spark the Royals' bats all series.

"He's a bit of a catalyst at the top of the order," Yost said. "More than anything else, he just raises his game this time of year because of his focus. He just intensifies his focus."

His offensive outbreak hadn't diminished his otherworldly defense, either.

Escobar's diving catch of Russell Martin's hit with runners on first and second in the second inning of Game 2 has become a postseason highlight-reel staple. He made an equally impressive dive to catch reliever Ryan Madson's throw for a force at second base.

"When I'm coming to the field every game in the postseason, my main thing is I want to win the game. I want to do the best I can," Escobar said. "And right now I'm really focused and I feel really good at home plate."∎

Kansas City Royals' Alex Gordon celebrates a solo home run off New York Mets relief pitcher Jeurys Familia during the ninth inning of Game 1. *AP Photo*

OCTOBER 27, 2015   KAUFFMAN STADIUM   KANSAS CITY, MISSOURI

KC ROYALS 5 • NY METS 4

HOSMER DELIVERS AS NEVER SAY DIE ROYALS WIN IN 14TH

Kansas City Royals starting pitcher Edinson Volquez (36) pitches against the New York Mets during Game 1. *AP Photo*

Eric Hosmer found a good way to atone for a run-scoring error in Game 1 of the World Series.

The first baseman's sacrifice fly in the 14th inning scored Alcides Escobar with the winning run, and the Kansas City Royals outlasted the New York Mets for a 5-4 victory.

Royals left fielder Alex Gordon homered with one out in the ninth to straightaway center on a 1-1 Jeurys Familia pitch to tie the game and send the 40,320 Kauffman Stadium crowd into complete bedlam and the game into extra innings.

"I was the happiest person in the stadium when Gordon homered," said Hosmer, whose eighth-inning error gave New York a 4-3 lead. "I told him, 'I just want to hug you right now.' I think a lot of people in Kansas City want to hug him."

Escobar reached on a throwing error by Mets third baseman David Wright to start the 14th. Second baseman Ben Zobrist, who had three hits, singled Escobar to third. After center fielder Lorenzo Cain was walked intentionally, Hosmer flied out to right, and Escobar beat Curtis Granderson's throw home.

"I just wanted another opportunity," Hosmer said. "It came down to me right then. I'm just happy for another chance."

Royals right-hander Chris Young worked three hitless innings, striking out four, to pick up the victory.

The 14-inning game matched the longest in World Series history. The contest lasted 5 hours, 9 minutes.

The Royals loaded the bases in the 12th but came away empty. Right fielder Paulo Orlando led off the inning with an infield single. Colon walked two intentionally before retiring designated hitter Jarrod Dyson on an easy fly ball to left.

New York led 3-1 after left fielder Michael Conforto hit a sacrifice fly in the sixth inning, but Kansas City scored twice in the bottom of the inning to tie the game. Hosmer's sacrifice fly cut New York's lead to 3-2, and third baseman Mike Moustakas leveled the score with a single to right-center.

Juan Lagares singled with two outs in the eighth, stole second and scored on Hosmer's error to give the Mets an abbreviated lead.

Lagares singled to center off Kelvin Herrera

Kansas City Royals shortstop Alcides Escobar (2) celebrates with second baseman Ben Zobrist (18) after hitting an inside-the-park home run during the first inning. *AP Photo*

Kansas City Royals first baseman Eric Hosmer (35) watches his game-winning sacrifice fly to right field with the bases loaded to win Game 1. *AP Photo*

Alcides Escobar (2) scores on a sacrifice fly by Eric Hosmer as New York Mets catcher Travis d'Arnaud reaches for the throw to home plate during the 14th inning. *AP Photo*

and swiped second. Wilmer Flores hit a grounder that Hosmer attempted to backhand, but the ball got past him for an error, allowing Lagares to come home. It was only the Royals' second error in 12 postseason games.

"It was a short hop, one of those in-between plays," Hosmer said. "No excuses. It was off my glove. I should have made the play."

Both starting pitchers, Mets right-hander Matt Harvey and Royals right-hander Edinson Volquez, threw six innings of three-run ball.

Volquez's father died of heart failure in the Dominican Republic before the game.

"I don't have any idea when he found out," Royals manager Ned Yost said. "We found out before the game, and the wishes of the family were to let Eddie pitch.

"He didn't know, and I guess after the game is when he found out."

Escobar, the MVP of the American League Championship Series after hitting .478 against Toronto, swung at the first pitch in the first inning, as his custom, but this swing produced World Series history. The shortstop drove a Matt Harvey 95 mph four-seam fastball to left center.

Mets center fielder Yoenis Cespedes attempted to make a backhand grab, but the ball ricocheted off his leg and into left field. By the time Conforto reversed his field and chased it down, Escobar circled the bases standing up.

It was the 10th inside-the-park home run in World Series history and the first since Mule Haas on Oct. 13, 1929, for the Philadelphia Athletics against the Chicago Cubs. ■

Royals players celebrate after Alcides Escobar scored on a sacrifice fly by Eric Hosmer during the 14th inning of Game 1.
AP Photo

BOX SCORE

	1	2	3	4	5	6	7	8	9	10	11	12	13	14	R	H	E
New York Mets	0	0	0	1	1	1	0	1	0	0	0	0	0	0	4	11	1
Kansas City	1	0	0	0	0	2	0	0	1	0	0	0	0	1	5	11	1

Mets	AB	R	H	RBI	BB	SO	LOB	AVG.
Granderson RF	5	1	1	1	2	0	0	.200
Wright 3B	7	0	2	0	0	2	4	.286
Murphy 2B	7	1	2	0	0	2	0	.286
Céspedes CF-LF	6	1	1	0	0	2	3	.167
Duda 1B	6	0	2	0	0	3	0	.333
d'Arnaud C	6	0	1	1	0	2	2	.167
Conforto LF	2	0	0	1	0	0	2	.000
Lagares CF	3	1	2	0	0	1	0	.667
Flores SS	4	0	0	0	1	0	3	.000
Johnson DH	1	0	0	0	0	0	0	.000
Cuddyer PH-DH	3	0	0	0	0	3	2	.000
Nieuwenhuis PH-DH	1	0	0	0	0	0	1	.000
Totals	51	4	11	3	3	15	17	

Royals	AB	R	H	RBI	BB	SO	LOB	AVG.
Escobar SS	6	2	1	1	0	0	2	.167
Zobrist 2B	6	1	3	0	1	0	0	.500
Cain CF	6	1	1	0	1	2	3	.167
Hosmer 1B	3	0	0	2	2	2	1	.000
K. Morales DH	3	0	0	0	1	1	2	.000
Dyson PR-DH	2	0	0	0	0	0	3	.000
Moustakas 3B	6	0	2	1	0	0	2	.333
Pérez C	6	0	2	0	0	0	2	.333
Gordon LF	5	1	1	1	1	2	2	.200
Rios RF	3	0	0	0	0	0	2	.000
Orlando RF	3	0	1	0	0	0	1	.333
Totals	49	5	11	5	6	7	20	

Mets	IP	H	R	ER	BB	SO	HR	ERA
Harvey	6.0	5	3	3	2	2	1	4.50
Reed	1.0	0	0	0	0	0	0	0.00
Clippard (H, 1)	0.2	1	0	0	1	2	0	0.00
Familia (B, 1)	1.1	1	1	1	0	0	1	6.75
Niese	2.0	1	0	0	0	3	0	0.00
Colón (L, 0-1)	2.1	3	1	0	3	0	0	0.00
Totals	13.1	11	5	4	6	7	2	

Royals	IP	H	R	ER	BB	SO	HR	ERA
Vólquez	6.0	6	3	3	1	3	1	4.50
Duffy	0.2	0	0	0	0	1	0	0.00
Herrera	1.1	3	1	0	0	2	0	0.00
Hochevar	1.0	1	0	0	0	0	0	0.00
Davis	1.0	0	0	0	0	3	0	0.00
Madson	1.0	1	0	0	1	2	0	0.00
Young (W, 1-0)	3.0	0	0	0	1	4	0	0.00
Totals	14.0	11	4	3	3	15	1	

Kansas City Royals shortstop Alcides Escobar (2) slides into home plate during Game 2. *AP Photo*

Inset: Escobar celebrates after scoring. *AP Photo*

OCTOBER 28, 2015   KAUFFMAN STADIUM   KANSAS CITY, MISSOURI
KC ROYALS 7   •   NY METS 1

CUETO PITCHES KC TO 2-0 SERIES LEAD

Kansas City Royals starting pitcher Johnny Cueto (47) pitched a complete game two-hitter. *AP Photo*

Johnny Cueto, who fluctuated between ghastly and grand in his first three postseason starts, pitched a two-hit complete game as the Kansas City Royals topped the New York Mets 7-1 Wednesday night to take a two-games-to-none lead in the World Series.

After an off day, the series switches to New York on Friday for Game 3.

Cueto, who was acquired in a July 26 trade with the Cincinnati Reds to be the ace the Royals were missing, was roughed up for eight runs while retiring only six Blue Jays in an American League Championship Series loss at Toronto on Oct. 19. That was Cueto at his worse.

Cueto, however, was at his best against the Mets, allowing only two singles by Mets first baseman Lucas Duda, and one did not leave the infield. The veteran right-hander, who retired 16 of the final 17 batters he faced, walked three and struck out four. He threw 122 pitches.

Kansas City Royals first baseman Eric Hosmer (35) dives into 3rd base ahead of the throw. *AP Photo*

The 40,410 fans in Kauffman Stadium were standing and serenading Cueto as he came out for the ninth inning, and they were screaming his name as the game ended.

"That's what they brought me here for, was to help win a World Series," Cueto said.

First baseman Eric Hosmer continues to be a RBI machine, driving in two Kansas City runs, bringing his RBI total to a postseason-leading 15. He has 27 RBIs in 28 career postseason games.

Shortstop Alcides Escobar continues to be a hit machine, contributing a single and a triple. He has hit safely in 12 consecutive postseason games, and his 21 hits the most in the majors this postseason.

"We don't swing and miss," Kansas City manager Ned Yost said. "We find ways to just keep putting the ball in play until you find holes."

The Royals batted around in a four-run fifth, scoring three runs with two outs to take a 4-1 lead.

Left fielder Alex Gordon led off the inning with a walk, and right fielder Alex Rios singled to left. After twice failing to put down a bunt, Escobar singled to center, scoring Gordon.

Mets right-hander Jacob deGrom retired the next two batters before Hosmer drilled a two-run single to center.

Hosmer moved to third on designated hitter Kendrys Morales single and scored on third baseman Mike Moustakas' single to right.

DeGrom, who was 3-0 with a 1.80 ERA in his first three postseason starts, labored through 38 pitches in the fifth and was pulled after five innings with his pitch count up to 94. He allowed four runs on six hits and three walks while striking out two. He was replaced by Hansel Robles in the sixth.

Two walks and a double play that was not

Kansas City Royals' Alex Gordon hits an RBI double during the eighth inning. *AP Photo*

turned helped the Mets score a run in the fourth. Cueto walked right fielder Curtis Granderson to lead off the inning and second baseman Daniel Murphy with one out.

Left fielder Yoenis Cespedes hit a grounder to Moustakas, who stepped on third to force out Granderson, but his throw to first pulled Hosmer's foot off the bag, allowing Cespedes to reach.

Duda made the Royals pay by slicing a single to left, scoring Murphy from second base.

The Royals padded their lead in the eighth with three runs off three Mets relievers. The inning included Gordon's run-producing double, an Escobar RBI triple and a Paulo Orlando sacrifice fly.∎

Royals catcher Salvador Perez, right, congratulates starting pitcher Johnny Cueto at the end of Game 2. *AP Photo*

BOX SCORE

	1	2	3	4	5	6	7	8	9	R	H	E
New York Mets	0	0	0	1	0	0	0	0	0	1	2	1
Kansas City	0	0	0	0	4	0	0	3	-	7	10	0

Mets	AB	R	H	RBI	BB	SO	LOB	AVG.
Granderson RF	3	0	0	0	1	0	0	.125
Wright 3B	4	0	0	0	0	0	1	.182
Murphy 2B	2	1	0	0	2	0	0	.222
Céspedes LF	4	0	0	0	0	1	3	.100
Duda 1B	3	0	2	1	0	0	0	.444
d'Arnaud C	3	0	0	0	0	0	3	.111
Conforto DH	3	0	0	0	0	1	0	.000
Flores SS	3	0	0	0	0	0	0	.000
Lagares CF	3	0	0	0	0	0	0	.333
Totals	28	1	2	1	3	4	7	

Mets	IP	H	R	ER	BB	SO	HR	ERA
deGrom (L, 0-1)	5.0	6	4	4	3	2	0	7.20
Robles	1.0	0	0	0	0	0	0	0.00
Niese	1.0	3	3	3	1	1	0	9.00
Reed	0.1	1	0	0	0	0	0	0.00
Gilmartin	0.2	0	0	0	0	0	0	0.00
Totals	8.0	10	7	7	4	3	0	

Royals	AB	R	H	RBI	BB	SO	LOB	AVG.
Escobar SS	5	1	2	2	0	0	1	.273
Zobrist 2B	5	0	0	0	0	0	3	.273
Cain CF	4	0	0	0	1	0	4	.100
Hosmer 1B	4	1	2	2	0	1	1	.286
K. Morales DH	4	0	1	0	0	1	3	.143
Moustakas 3B	3	1	2	1	1	0	0	.444
Pérez C	4	1	1	0	0	0	5	.300
Gordon LF	2	2	1	1	2	0	0	.286
Rios RF	3	1	1	0	0	1	1	.167
Orlando RF	0	0	0	1	0	0	0	.333
Totals	34	7	10	7	4	3	18	

Royals	IP	H	R	ER	BB	SO	HR	ERA
Cueto (W, 1-0)	9.0	2	1	1	3	4	0	1.00
Totals	9.0	2	1	1	3	4	0	

Kansas City Royals first baseman Eric Hosmer is ready for action at first base. *AP Photo*

HOSMER COMING OF AGE

Royals skipper Ned Yost watched as baseballs begin knocking into the outfield wall on a sun drenched afternoon at Kaufmann Stadium.

Eric Hosmer might be the last player anyone would expect to take optional batting practice, but that's why he's among the best hitters in baseball.

"He works hard," manager Ned Yost said. "That home run he hit last night (No. 12, an opposite-field two-run shot in the first inning of Kansas City's 6-1 victory) was something else.

"He has so much power to the opposite field," Yost said of Hosmer. "That's the hardest kind of power to have. Everybody's got a little pull power, but to drive a ball out to center field like he did? He's impressive. He's made himself a complete hitter."

Across baseball, offensive numbers are down. Hosmer, though, is trending up. Way up. Hosmer hit only nine homers last season but found new life in the playoffs and hasn't stopped hitting since.

At 25, Hosmer is still young, but he also is experienced. This is his fifth season in the big leagues, and he's been the driving force behind the Royals' early success.

"I'm definitely in a good place right now," said Hosmer. "In certain counts, I'm definitely taking more chances and trying to not miss them and starting my (load) a little earlier."

He has won back-to-back Gold Gloves at first base, and he continues to make plays that even surprise his manager and teammates.

"You see a ball hit and think it's heading to right field," Yost said, "and Hoz snags it. He makes the plays he's supposed to make and the plays he's not supposed to make."

Added all-star shortstop Alcides Escobar, who has a cannon of an arm: "If you get the throw

AP Photo

anywhere near Hoz at first base, he's going to catch it. He's the best, man."

In the same fashion George Brett grew from a timid rookie to the voice of the team, Hosmer has accepted the torch from the Hall of Fame third baseman and is now the face of the hottest team in the American League.

"We're still hungry, still scrapping for wins," said Hosmer, who ranks fourth in batting average (.317), tied for fifth in multi-hit games (38), tied for fifth in hits (131) and seventh in on-base percentage (.376).

Hosmer is the man every young woman in Kansas City wants to marry, and the guy every dad dreams of his daughter dating. He has the movie star good looks and personality of a budding superstar who feels comfortable in Kansas City.

"The young guys on this team all came up together and we wanted to give something special to the fans who have waited so long to get back to the postseason," Hosmer said, referring to the team's remarkable run to the World Series in 2014. "Hopefully we can get back there and finish the job this year." ▪

Kansas City Royals' Alcides Escobar (2) gets out of the way of a high pitch during the first inning. *AP Photo*

OCTOBER 30, 2015   CITI FIELD   NEW YORK, NEW YORK

KC ROYALS 3 • NY METS 9

NEW YORK BATS COME ALIVE IN GAME 3 WIN

New York Mets third baseman David Wright (5) rounds the bases as he hit a two run homer after Kansas City Royals starting pitcher Yordano Ventura (30) reacts during the first inning.   *AP Photo*

First Noah Syndergaard intimidated the Kansas City Royals. Then the New York Mets beat the Royals at their own game.

The World Series just got serious.

Syndergaard threw six strong innings after sailing his first pitch at the head of Royals shortstop Alcides Escobar and the Mets scored multiple runs in three innings on their way to a 9-3 win in Game 3 of the World Series at Citi Field.

With the victory, the Mets narrowed the Royals' lead to two games to one. Game 4 is scheduled for Saturday night — and if Syndergaard's words late Friday night are any indication, the intensity will be ratcheted up beyond the usual levels associated with a World Series.

"My intent on that pitch was to make them

Kansas City Royals second baseman Ben Zobrist (18) points to the sky after pulling into second with a double during the first inning. *AP Photo*

New York Mets' Michael Conforto is safe at first as Kansas City Royals' Eric Hosmer makes a diving attempt during the fourth inning. *AP Photo*

uncomfortable," Syndergaard said of his pitch at Escobar, who is known for swinging at the first pitch and won the AL Championship Series MVP after hitting .386 in the six-game win over the Toronto Blue Jays. "And I think I did just that."

Royals third baseman Mike Moustakas was captured by television cameras yelling obscenities at Syndergaard.

Syndergaard's reaction?

"If they have a problem with me throwing inside, then they can meet me 60 feet, six inches away," Syndergaard said. "I've got no problem with that."

While Syndergaard set the early message, it was the Royals who got off to a fast start. After Escobar struck out on four pitches, second baseman Ben Zobrist doubled, went to third on a single by center fielder Lorenzo Cain and scored when the Mets could not complete a double play on first baseman Eric Hosmer's grounder to first.

Mets third baseman David Wright (2-for-5, four RBIs) hit a two-run homer in the bottom of the inning, but the Royals scored twice in the second, when they opened the inning with three straight singles. The third, by Rios, tied the score and Rios raced home with the go-ahead run on a wild pitch by Syndergaard.

But the Mets' lanky rookie stranded Escobar at second by retiring Zobrist on a flyout — the first of 12 straight outs by Syndergaard.

Syndergaard helped the Mets regain the lead in the bottom of the third, when he delivered a leadoff single and scored on a homer to right by right fielder Curtis Granderson.

The first three Mets to step to the plate in the fourth all reached base, though they scored just once on an RBI single by left fielder Michael Conforto. After Syndergaard escaped a bases-loaded jam in the top of the sixth, New York put the game away by batting around and scoring four runs on four singles in the bottom half.

The Royals had 21 hits and three multi-run innings in winning the first two games in Kansas City.

Syndergaard ended up allowing three runs, seven hits and two walks while striking out six. The Royals struck out just 10 times in the first two games, including only four times against Mets starters Matt Harvey and Jacob deGrom.

"We swung the bat really good against him in the first two innings," Royals manager Ned Yost said. "If you're going to get a really good pitcher, you better get him early."

A trio of Mets relievers set down the final nine Royals in order. For only the second time in 13 playoff games, no Kansas City player had multiple hits.

Right-hander Yordano Ventura took the loss for the Royals after allowing five runs, seven hits and no walks while striking out one in 3 1/3 innings.∎

Kansas City Royals catcher Salvador Perez has his bat shattered by New York Mets starting pitcher Noah Syndergaard. *AP Photo*

BOX SCORE

	1	2	3	4	5	6	7	8	9	R	H	E
Kansas City	1	2	0	0	0	0	0	0	0	3	7	0
New York Mets	2	0	2	1	0	4	0	0	-	9	12	0

Royals	AB	R	H	RBI	BB	SO	LOB	AVG.
Escobar SS	4	0	1	0	0	2	0	.267
Zobrist 2B	4	1	1	0	0	0	1	.267
Cain CF	4	0	1	0	0	1	0	.143
Hosmer 1B	4	0	0	1	0	1	1	.182
Moustakas 3B	4	0	1	0	0	0	1	.385
Pérez C	3	1	1	0	1	0	0	.308
Gordon LF	3	0	1	0	1	2	0	.300
Rios RF	3	1	1	1	0	0	3	.222
Herrera P	0	0	0	0	0	0	0	.000
Madson P	0	0	0	0	0	0	0	.000
Medlen P	0	0	0	0	0	0	0	.000
K. Morales PH	1	0	0	0	0	0	0	.125
Ventura P	0	0	0	0	0	0	0	.000
Duffy P	0	0	0	0	0	0	0	.000
Mondesi PH	1	0	0	0	0	1	0	.000
Hochevar P	0	0	0	0	0	0	0	.000
F. Morales P	0	0	0	0	0	0	0	.000
Orlando RF	1	0	0	0	0	0	0	.250
Totals	32	3	7	2	2	7	6	

Mets	AB	R	H	RBI	BB	SO	LOB	AVG.
Granderson RF	5	3	2	2	0	0	4	.231
Wright 3B	5	1	2	4	0	2	0	.250
Murphy 2B	4	0	0	0	1	1	0	.154
Céspedes CF-LF	3	0	1	1	0	1	0	.154
Duda 1B	4	1	1	0	0	2	3	.385
d'Arnaud C	4	0	2	0	0	0	0	.231
Conforto LF	2	0	1	1	0	0	0	.143
Lagares PH-CF	2	1	1	0	0	0	1	.375
Flores SS	3	1	0	0	0	0	3	.000
Syndergaard P	2	1	1	0	0	1	2	.500
Uribe PH	1	1	1	1	0	0	0	1.000
Reed P	0	0	0	0	0	0	0	.000
Nieuwenhuis PH	1	0	0	0	0	1	1	.000
Clippard P	0	0	0	0	0	0	0	.000
Familia P	0	0	0	0	0	0	0	.000
Totals	36	9	12	9	1	8	14	

Royals	IP	H	R	ER	BB	SO	HR	ERA
Ventura (L, 0-1)	3.1	7	5	5	0	1	2	13.50
Duffy	0.2	0	0	0	0	1	0	0.00
Hochevar	1.0	1	0	0	0	2	0	0.00
F. Morales	0.1	2	4	4	0	0	0	108.00
Herrera	0.2	1	0	0	1	1	0	0.00
Madson	1.0	1	0	0	0	1	0	0.00
Medlen	1.0	0	0	0	0	2	0	0.00
Totals	8.0	12	9	9	1	8	2	

Mets	IP	H	R	ER	BB	SO	HR	ERA
Syndergaard (W, 1-0)	6.0	7	3	3	2	6	0	4.50
Reed	1.0	0	0	0	0	0	0	0.00
Clippard	1.0	0	0	0	0	0	0	0.00
Familia	1.0	0	0	0	0	1	0	3.86
Totals	9.0	7	3	3	2	7	0	

Alex Gordon hits an RBI single in the fifth inning. *AP Photo*

OCTOBER 31, 2015   CITI FIELD   NEW YORK, NEW YORK

KC ROYALS 5 • NY METS 3

LATE RALLY LIFTS ROYALS

Kansas City Royals starting pitcher Chris Young (32) in action during Game 4.   *AP Photo*

On a night when America was getting set to turn their clocks back, the Kansas City Royals are within one win of setting their clock back all the way to 1985.

Third baseman Mike Moustakas' tiebreaking RBI single highlighted a three-run eighth inning Saturday night that lifted the Royals to a 5-3 win over the Mets in Game 4 and a three-games-to-one lead in the World Series. Kansas City will look to clinch its first championship since 1985 on Sunday at Citi Field.

"We've put ourselves in a good spot," Royals first baseman Eric Hosmer said. "But at the same time, they've got a lot of tough arms. We've just got to find a way to get it done one more time."

The Mets carried a 3-2 lead into the eighth

thanks to two solo homers by rookie left fielder Michael Conforto and a sacrifice fly by right fielder Curtis Granderson — and were five outs from evening the Series when the Royals did what they seemingly do all the time: mount a comeback in a deceptively slow fashion.

Second baseman Ben Zobrist and center fielder Lorenzo Cain each drew one-out walks against Mets right-hander Tyler Clippard. Right-hander Jeurys Familia, New York's closer, entered and induced Hosmer to hit a slow grounder to second.

But the ball went under the glove of Daniel Murphy and dribbled into shallow right field as Zobrist scored the tying run and Cain raced to third.

"It's a team that just looks for a little crack," Royals manager Ned Yost said. "If we find a little crack, they're going to make something happen. It's amazing how they do that."

Moustakas followed with a single to right to score Cain and catcher Salvador Perez singled to right — his third hit of the game — to bring home Hosmer with an insurance run.

"We're just trying to put the ball in play against a guy like Familia," Moustakas said. "And 'Hoz' did a good job of putting the ball in play and making some things happen."

Kansas City Royals' Salvador Perez reacts after hitting an RBI single during the eighth inning. *AP Photo*

In a play never to be forgotten by Mets fans, second baseman Daniel Murphy (28) boots a slow roller during the eighth inning that allows Ben Zobrist to race home with the tying run. The Royals went on to score two more runs in the inning on their way to another come from behind win. *AP Photo*

Alcides Escobar (2) and Eric Hosmer (35) celebrating in the 8th. *AP Photo*

Lorenzo Cain (6) dives for third base after a throwing error on a pickoff attempt by New York Mets starting pitcher Bartolo Colon during the sixth inning. *AP Photo*

Mets manager Terry Collins said he had no regrets starting the eighth with Clippard, who has a 6.98 ERA in his last 20 appearances dating to Sept. 6.

"We said before the inning, if the go-ahead run gets on, we're going to go to Familia," Collins said. "I didn't want to burn Jeurys tonight for two innings if I could help it. So it didn't work."

Left fielder Alex Gordon (fifth inning) and Cain (sixth inning) had RBI singles for the Royals, who have won five games this postseason in which they trailed by at least two runs. That ties a record set by the 1996 New York Yankees, who won the World Series.

"I think everyone would feel a lot better if we just stayed tied with that record and came out

tomorrow and (got) a nice lead, a nice cushion," Hosmer said with a laugh. "We've been through enough crazy games this postseason."

Five Royals pitchers combined on the six-hitter. Right-hander Chris Young started and gave up two runs, two hits and one walk while striking out three in four innings.

Right-hander Ryan Madson picked up the win with a perfect seventh and right-hander Wade Davis notched his first save of the Series and his fourth of the playoffs by getting the final six outs. ■

Kansas City Royals second baseman Ben Zobrist waits to tag out New York Mets' Curtis Granderson (3) as he attempts to steal second base during the fifth inning   *AP Photo*

BOX SCORE

	1	2	3	4	5	6	7	8	9	R	H	E
Kansas City	0	0	0	0	1	1	0	3	0	5	9	0
New York Mets	0	0	2	0	1	0	0	0	0	3	6	2

Royals	AB	R	H	RBI	BB	SO	LOB	AVG.
Escobar SS	5	0	1	0	0	0	2	.250
Zobrist 2B	3	2	1	0	1	2	1	.278
Cain CF	3	1	1	1	1	1	0	.176
Hosmer 1B	4	1	0	0	0	1	2	.133
Moustakas 3B	4	0	1	1	0	0	1	.353
Pérez C	4	1	3	1	0	1	1	.412
Gordon LF	4	0	1	1	0	0	3	.286
Rios RF	3	0	0	0	0	0	1	.167
Orlando RF	1	0	0	0	0	1	0	.200
Young P	1	0	0	0	0	1	0	.000
K. Morales PH	1	0	1	0	0	0	0	.222
Duffy P	0	0	0	0	0	0	0	.000
Hochevar P	0	0	0	0	0	0	0	.000
Dyson PH	1	0	0	0	0	1	0	.000
Madson P	0	0	0	0	0	0	0	.000
Davis P	1	0	0	0	0	1	0	.000
Totals	35	5	9	4	2	9	11	

Mets	AB	R	H	RBI	BB	SO	LOB	AVG.
Granderson RF	3	0	1	1	0	0	0	.250
Wright 3B	3	0	0	0	1	1	0	.211
Murphy 2B	4	0	1	0	0	0	1	.176
Céspedes CF-LF	4	0	1	0	0	2	0	.176
Duda 1B	4	0	0	0	0	1	2	.294
d'Arnaud C	3	0	0	0	0	1	0	.188
Conforto LF	3	2	2	2	0	1	0	.300
Clippard P	0	0	0	0	0	0	0	.000
Familia P	0	0	0	0	0	0	0	.000
Nieuwenhuis CF	0	0	0	0	0	0	0	.000
Flores SS	3	1	1	0	0	2	0	.077
Matz P	1	0	0	0	0	0	0	.000
Niese P	0	0	0	0	0	0	0	.000
Colón P	0	0	0	0	0	0	0	.000
Reed P	0	0	0	0	0	0	0	.000
Lagares CF	0	0	0	0	0	0	0	.375
Johnson PH	1	0	0	0	0	0	0	.000
Robles P	0	0	0	0	0	0	0	.000
Totals	36	9	12	9	1	8	14	

Royals	IP	H	R	ER	BB	SO	HR	ERA
Young	4.0	2	2	2	1	3	1	2.57
Duffy	1.0	2	1	1	0	1	1	3.86
Hochevar	1.0	0	0	0	0	0	0	0.00
Madson (W, 1-0)	1.0	0	0	0	0	2	0	0.00
Davis (S, 1)	2.0	2	0	0	0	2	0	0.00
Totals	9.0	6	3	3	1	8	2	

Mets	IP	H	R	ER	BB	SO	HR	ERA
Matz	5.0	7	2	2	0	5	0	3.60
Niese (H, 1)	0.2	0	0	0	0	0	0	7.36
Colón (H, 1)	0.1	0	0	0	0	1	0	0.00
Reed (H, 1)	1.0	0	0	0	0	1	0	0.00
Clippard (L, 0-1; H, 2)	0.1	0	2	2	2	0	0	9.00
Familia (B, 2)	0.2	2	1	0	0	0	0	3.00
Robles	1.0	0	0	0	0	2	0	0.00
Totals	9.0	9	5	4	2	9	0	

Kansas City Royals' Eric Hosmer hits a RBI single off New York Mets starting pitcher Matt Harvey during the ninth inning of Game 5. *AP Photo*

NOVEMBER 1, 2015   CITI FIELD   NEW YORK, NEW YORK
KC ROYALS 7 • NY METS 2

ROYALS WIN FIRST WORLD SERIES CHAMPIONSHIP IN 30 YEARS

For the first time since 1985, the Kansas City Royals are world champions.

The Royals came back from a two-run deficit in the top of the ninth inning of Game 5 on Sunday night before pinch hitter Christian Colon laced a tiebreaking single in the top of the 12th inning as Kansas City beat the New York Mets 7-2.

Shortstop Alcides Escobar hit an RBI double and center fielder Lorenzo Cain added a three-run double later in the 12th for the Royals, who won a record seven postseason games in which they trailed by at least two runs.

Right-hander Luke Hochevar threw two hitless innings for the win before right-hander Wade Davis struck out three in the bottom of the 12th to seal the win.

Davis fanned shortstop Wilmer Flores and flung his glove in the air to set off a wild celebration at the pitcher's mound by the Royals, who became the first team to win the World Series the year after losing it since the 1989 Oakland Athletics.

Hundreds of Royals fans dressed in blue descended toward the Kansas City dugout to cheer their champs.

"I couldn't have written a better script," manager Ned Yost said.

Meanwhile, the Mets must wait 'til next year to win their first championship since 1986.

In between championships, the Royals

New York Mets catcher Travis d'Arnaud watches as Kansas City Royals' Lorenzo Cain (6) signals to Eric Hosmer after Hosmer's RBI double.   *AP Photo*

experienced 20 losing seasons, served as the poster boys for the supposed chasm between big and small markets and became a popular punch line for professional futility.

The Royals finally ended the three-decade championship drought with a consistent contact, keep the line moving approach. The strikeout is

Home plate umpire Alfonso Marquez watches as Kansas City Royals' Eric Hosmer (35) scores past New York Mets catcher Travis d'Arnaud during the ninth inning tying up the game. *AP Photo*

Kansas City Royals' Christian Colon watches his RBI single off New York Mets relief pitcher Addison Reed during the 12th inning of Game 5. *AP Photo*

more accepted now than ever, but Kansas City wore down opposing teams with a grinding, aggressive, one-through-25 approach built on putting the ball in play.

That is what the Royals did in building the winning rally in the 12th as well as the game-tying rally in the ninth.

World Series MVP Salvador Perez led off the 12th with a single down the right field line against right-hander Addison Reed. Pinch runner Jarrod Dyson stole second and went to third on a groundout by left fielder Alex Gordon before trotting home on the hit by Colon, who was batting for the first time this postseason.

The Royals forced extra innings in the ninth against Mets right-hander Matt Harvey, who shut Kansas City out on just four hits through eight innings while being serenaded with chants of "HAR-VEY! HAR-VEY!" from the sellout crowd of 44,859.

"Going into the ninth, I felt great," Harvey said. "I felt like my mechanics, everything was right where I wanted it to be.

Harvey, who sprinted to the mound to a standing ovation in the ninth inning, walked the leadoff batter, Cain, who promptly stole second.

Cain scored on a double to left by first baseman Eric Hosmer.

"If you're going to let him just face one guy, you shouldn't have sent him out there," Mets manager Terry Collins said about the decision not to lift Harvey after the leadoff walk. "When the double [was] hit, that's when I said, 'I've got to see if we can get out of this with only one run.' And it didn't work. It was my fault."

Harvey was pulled for right-hander Jeurys Familia, who retired third baseman Mike Moustakas on a grounder that moved Hosmer to third. With the infield in, Perez grounded to third. Mets third baseman David Wright looked back Hosmer and fired to first, but Hosmer broke for home with the ball in the air.

First baseman Lucas Duda threw home, but the throw was wild as Hosmer slid home with the tying run. Familia is the first pitcher to be charged with three blown saves in the same World Series.

The Mets took the 2-0 lead on a first-inning leadoff homer by right fielder Curtis Granderson and a sixth-inning sacrifice fly by Duda.

Royals right-hander Edinson Volquez, pitching about 24 hours after he returned from attending his father's funeral, allowed two runs (one earned)

Jarrod Dyson (1) races home with the go ahead run in the 12th inning. *AP Photo*

on two hits and five walks while striking out five over six innings.

The Royals became the first team since the 2002 Angels to come from behind in all four World Series wins, according to STATS. That's how they washed away the bitter taste of last year's Game 7 loss at home to San Francisco, an October heartbreak that drove them to their singular focus all season.

Never waver. Win it all this time.

"We never quit. We never put our heads down," Perez said. "We always compete to the last out."

Now, this group of homegrown favorites that turned around a floundering franchise, Mike Moustakas and Alex Gordon and Hosmer, can take their place in Royals history alongside George Brett, Willie Wilson, Bret Saberhagen and those champs from 30 years ago. ∎

Lorenzo Cain (6) drills a three-run double in the 12th to break open the game. *AP Photo*

BOX SCORE

	1	2	3	4	5	6	7	8	9	10	11	12	R	H	E
Kansas City	0	0	0	0	0	0	0	0	2	0	0	5	7	10	1
New York Mets	1	0	0	0	0	1	0	0	0	0	0	0	2	4	2

Royals	AB	R	H	RBI	BB	SO	LOB	AVG.
Escobar SS	6	1	1	1	0	2	1	.231
Zobrist 2B	5	1	1	0	1	0	0	.261
Cain CF	5	1	2	3	1	2	1	.227
Hosmer 1B	6	1	2	1	0	2	3	.190
Moustakas 3B	6	0	1	0	0	1	3	.304
Pérez C	5	0	1	1	0	1	2	.364
Dyson PR	0	1	0	0	0	0	0	.000
Butera C	0	0	0	0	0	0	0	.000
Gordon LF	4	0	0	0	1	0	3	.222
Rios RF	3	0	0	0	0	1	3	.133
Herrera P	0	0	0	0	0	0	0	.000
K. Morales PH	1	0	0	0	0	1	0	.200
Hochevar P	0	0	0	0	0	0	0	.000
Colón PH	1	1	1	0	0	0	0	1.000
Davis P	0	0	0	0	0	0	0	.000
Vólquez P	2	0	1	0	0	1	1	.500
Orlando RF	3	1	0	0	0	0	1	.125
Totals	47	7	10	7	3	11	18	

Royals	IP	H	R	ER	BB	SO	HR	ERA
Vólquez	6.0	2	2	1	5	5	1	3.00
Herrera	3.0	1	0	0	0	3	0	0.00
Hochevar (W, 1-0)	2.0	0	0	0	1	0	0	0.00
Davis	1.0	1	0	0	0	3	0	0.00
Totals	12.0	4	2	1	6	11	1	

Mets	AB	R	H	RBI	BB	SO	LOB	AVG.
Granderson RF	4	2	1	1	1	2	0	.250
Wright 3B	5	0	1	0	0	3	0	.208
Murphy 2B	3	0	0	0	2	2	2	.150
Céspedes CF	3	0	0	0	0	0	4	.150
Lagares CF	2	0	0	0	0	0	1	.300
Duda 1B	2	0	0	1	2	1	0	.263
d'Arnaud C	5	0	0	0	0	1	4	.143
Conforto LF	5	0	2	0	0	1	1	.333
Flores SS	4	0	0	0	1	1	2	.059
Harvey P	3	0	0	0	0	0	2	.000
Familia P 0	0	0	0	0	0	0	0	.000
Johnson PH	1	0	0	0	0	0	0	.000
Niese P	0	0	0	0	0	0	0	.000
Reed P	0	0	0	0	0	0	0	.000
Colón P	0	0	0	0	0	0	0	.000
Totals	37	2	4	2	6	11	16	

Mets	IP	H	R	ER	BB	SO	HR	ERA
Harvey	8.0	5	2	2	2	9	0	3.21
Familia (BS, 3)	2.0	0	0	0	0	2	0	1.80
Niese	1.0	1	0	0	0	0	0	5.79
Reed (L, 0-1)	0.1	3	5	4	1	0	0	9.82
Colón	0.2	1	0	0	0	0	0	0.00
Totals	12.0	10	7	6	3	11	0	

Royals reliever Wade Davis (17) reacts after striking out the Mets Wilmer Flores (4) for the final out. *AP Photo*

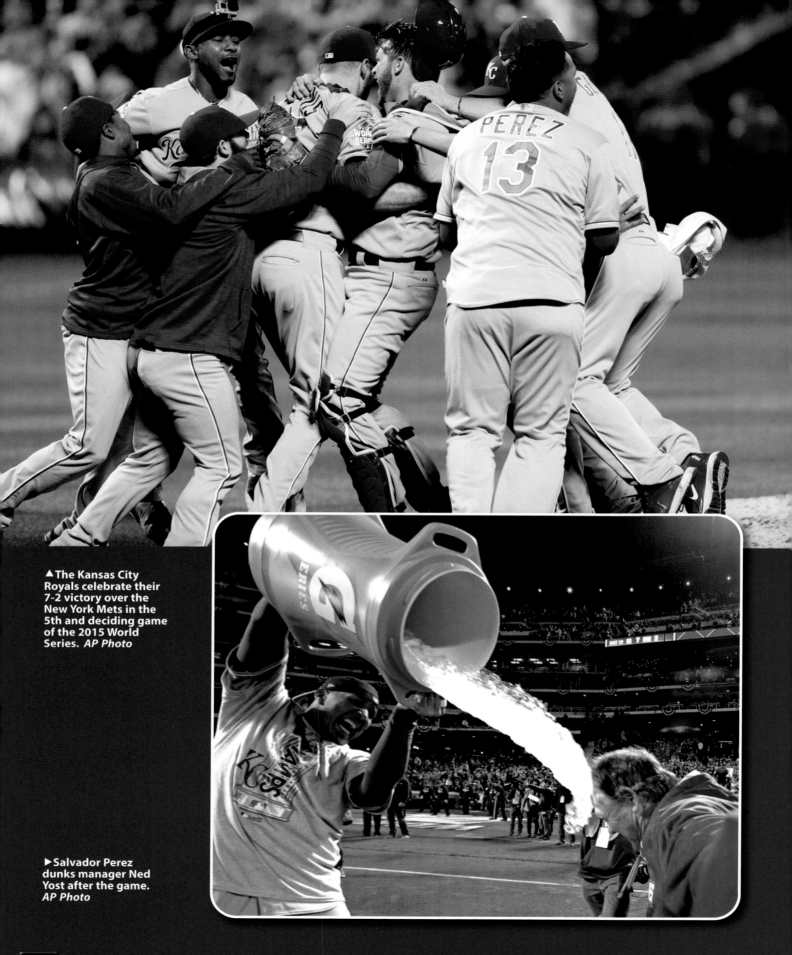

▲The Kansas City Royals celebrate their 7-2 victory over the New York Mets in the 5th and deciding game of the 2015 World Series. *AP Photo*

▶Salvador Perez dunks manager Ned Yost after the game. *AP Photo*

PEREZ NAMED WORLD SERIES MVP

After the Kansas City Royals sealed their 7-2 victory in Game 5 of the World Series over the New York Mets, Royals catcher Salvador Perez was unanimously named the Most Valuable Player of the 2015 World Series.

Perez hit .364/.391/.455 in the series, going 8-for-22 at the plate with two doubles while scoring three runs with two RBIs. In the Series-clinching win, Perez plated the tying run in the Royals' ninth-inning comeback, then sparked their victory in the 12th inning with a leadoff single down the right-field line before being lifted for pinch runner Jarrod Dyson.

"He just had a phenomenal series," said Royals manager Ned Yost. "I think if I had one regret during the whole playoffs, [it] was I had to pinch run for Sal there in that inning. But it opened up the door for us to score five. I really wish that Sal could have been out there to jump in [closer Wade Davis'] arms when we got the final out."

Up to that point, Perez had caught every inning for the Royals in the series, but at times was nearly forced out of games by injuries that are the routine hazards of catchers at every level.

"What I always say, I think it's part of my job," Perez said. "Take a foul ball, a wild pitch."

In Game 5, batting against Mets closer Jeurys Familia with Eric Hosmer on third base and one out, it was Perez's grounder to third base that allowed Hosmer to score. The Royals' first baseman scampered home, forcing an errant throw by Mets first baseman Lucas Duda after Perez was retired on third baseman David Wright's assist.

"You guys know what we've done all season," Perez said. "We never quit. We never put our heads down. ... We always compete to the last out. And that's what we did tonight." ∎

Salvador Perez poses with his World Series MVP trophy along with the new car he received for being named MVP. *AP Photo*

Kansas City Royals pose with the World Series trophy after winning 7-2 in 12th innings. *AP Photo*

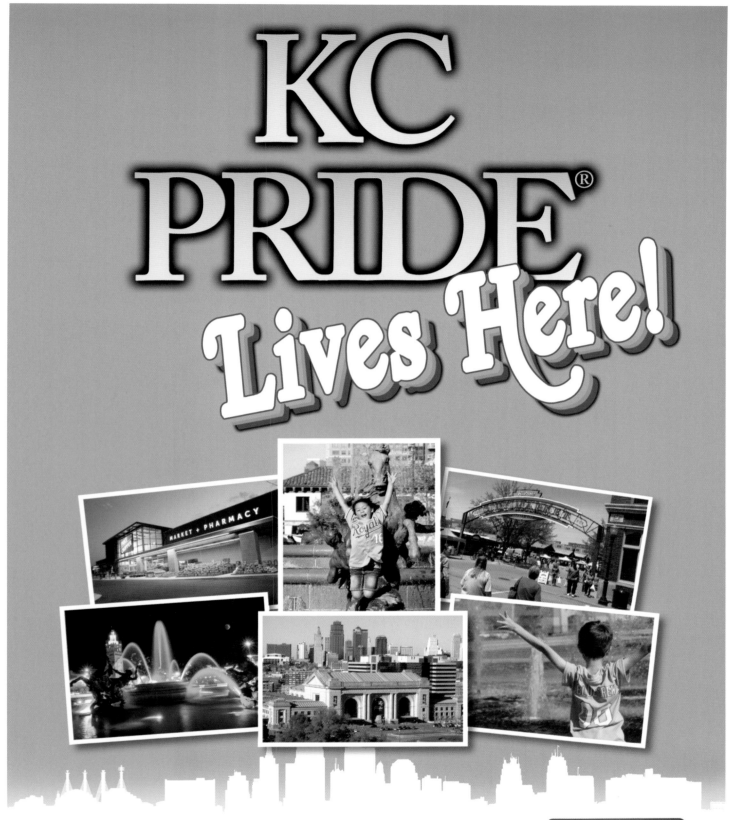

KC PRIDE®
Lives Here!

Your 50 locally owned Price Chopper stores are proud to have been part of our great city for 35 years! We're celebrating 2015 as one of the very best ever.

128